sta.
1994.

FEARON'S

Practical Mathematics for Consumers

SECOND EDITION

Carol Staudacher
Steve Turner

Globe Fearon Educational Publisher
Paramus, New Jersey

Paramount Publishing

Pacemaker Curriculum Advisor: Stephen C. Larsen
Stephen C. Larsen holds a B.S. and an M.S. in Speech Pathology from the University of
Nebraska at Omaha, and an Ed.D. in Learning Disabilities from the University of Kansas. In
the course of his career, Dr. Larsen has worked in the Teacher Corps on a Nebraska Indian
Reservation, as a Fullbright senior lecturer in Portugal and Spain, and as a speech pathologist
in the public schools. A full professor at the University of Texas at Austin, he has nearly twenty
years' experience as a teacher trainer on the university level. He is the author of sixty journal
articles, three textbooks, and six widely used standardized tests including the Test of Written
Learning (TOWL) and the Test of Adolescent Language (TOAL).

Subject Area Consultant: Helen Butler Miller
Helen Butler Miller holds an M.S. in Mathematics from California State University, Hayward,
California. She has taught various math courses as a fulltime instructor at Diablo Valley
College, Pleasant Hill, California.

Second Edition Consultant: Ronn Yablun
Ronn Yablun holds a B.S. from Northern Illinois University. He is chairman of the math
department at Northridge Junior High School in California. He is also the founder of
Mathamazement, a learning center for remediation and enrichment in math.

Editors: Emily Hutchinson, Nan Bostick
Contributing Editor: Sharon Wheeler
Text Design: Michelle Taverniti
Cover Design: Marc Ong, Side by Side Studios
Illustrator: Duane Bibby
Production Manager: Teresa A. Holden
Graphics Coordinator: Joe C. Shines
Graphics Production: Karen Coggeshall
Photo Credits: Rose Skytta/Jeroboam, Inc. 2; Laimute Druskis/Jeroboam, Inc. 16, 52, 222;
John Herr 36, 70, 86, 120, 136, 240, 254; Michael Rothstein/Jeroboam, Inc. 104, 206; Emilio
Mercado/Jeroboam, Inc. 172, 286; Jane Scherr/Jeroboam, Inc. 188; Gregg Mancuso/
Jeroboam, Inc. 272.

About the Cover Photograph: *Kathleen Campbell/AllStock.* Mathematics has many practical
applications, from balancing one's checkbook to getting the best prices at the produce market.
To find out how smart shoppers use math at the grocery store, see Chapter 9.

ISBN 0–8224–6900–6

Printed in the United States of America
3. 10 9 8 7 6 5 4 3 2 1
Cover Printer/NEBC
DO

CONTENTS

A Note to the Student

In all areas of life, it's not what you know that counts—it's what you can *do* with what you know. Think about it. You probably already know how to add, subtract, multiply, and divide. But how well can you use those skills outside the classroom? Or to put it another way, can you *apply* what you know to real life problems and challenges?

That's what this book is all about. Practical Mathematics is math with a purpose. In these pages you'll find important information about buying, saving, and spending. You'll learn how to read a paycheck stub and a checking account statement. You'll learn how to make wise purchases when you shop for groceries or clothes or furniture. By the time you finish this book, you'll know about loans and interest, credit cards, and insurance. You'll be able to make a budget, compare car prices, and plan a vacation you can afford. In short, you will be able to "think math" when you need to make a plan or get a job done. This ability will help you avoid many mistakes and problems. It will help you make good decisions all your life—at school, at home, and on the job.

Throughout the book you'll find notes in the margins of the pages. These friendly notes are there to make you stop and think. Sometimes they comment on the material you are learning. Sometimes they remind you of something you already know. And sometimes they give you tips, examples, and helpful hints.

You will also find several study aids in the book. At the beginning of every chapter, you'll find **Learning Objectives**. They will help you focus on the important points covered in the chapter. **Words to Know** are also in the beginning of each chapter. They give you a look ahead at the vocabulary you may find difficult. The **Basics Practice** boxes in the margins will help you brush up on the fundamentals of arithmetic. At the end of each chapter, a **Summary** will give you a quick review of what you've just learned.

Everyone who put this book together worked hard to make it useful, interesting, and enjoyable. The rest is up to you. We wish you well in your studies. Our success is in your accomplishment.

Unit One

On Your Own

1 Covering Your Expenses

Living on your own brings new responsibilities as well as privileges.

Chapter Learning Objectives

- List essential living expenses.
- Tell the difference between wants and needs.
- Prepare and analyze a three-day personal expense record.
- Identify examples of fixed and variable expenses.
- Calculate and compare spending in various categories, such as groceries.
- Review basic math skills in the Appendix at the back of this textbook.

Words to Know

expenses   money spent on various things that are needed or wanted; costs

fixed   unchanging; remaining the same

income   money received for working, or from investments or other sources

insurance   protection against losses or damage

outgo   money paid out for expenses

utilities   services such as electricity, gas, water, and garbage pickup

variable   changing from time to time

Going Out on Your Own?

You are going to rent a room or share a place with a friend. Maybe you're getting your own apartment.

Going out on your own means you'll have the freedom to make your own choices. Along with that freedom, you need to be able to take care of yourself. This means taking care of your own needs.

You need to eat. So the money you spend on groceries is covering a need. You need heat, electricity, and water. You must pay for these **utilities**. They are needs, like the rent that you'll pay for the place where you live.

You will also have certain wants. Sometimes what you need and what you want will be the same. But sometimes they will be different.

You may want a tuna fish sandwich for lunch. You need to eat lunch, so your needs and your wants are the same.

You may want to see a movie on Saturday night. This is fine, if you can afford it. But seeing a movie is not something you need, like food and water.

To get clear about wants and needs, Sandy made a list of the money she spent for a week. Every time she bought something, she wrote it down. Next to it, she wrote the cost.

At the end of the week, this is what Sandy's list looked like:

Purchase	Cost
bike repair	$10.50
sweater	40.65
toothpaste	2.17
pizza at Rudolpho's	8.50
movie	4.00
repay a loan	5.00
groceries	12.50
fingernail polish	4.00

Progress Check 1

Make two lists on separate sheets of paper. On one list, write down the things you think Sandy needed to have or do. On the second list, write down the things you think Sandy wanted but didn't really need. Include the costs of each thing on each list. Use your two lists to answer these questions.

1. Did Sandy spend more on the things she needed or on the things she wanted? How much more?
2. Name two items from Sandy's list that she could have gone without to save $12.50 for next week's groceries.

Wordwise: *Afford* means to have the money, time, or strength for something. In this chapter, *afford* means to have the money.

Did You Know? If you buy a 50¢ snack every other day for a year, you will spend $91.

How Do You Really Spend Your Money?

Now think about all the different things you've spent money on in the last three days. Don't leave anything out. Did you buy your lunch? Did you get a soda or donut? Did you put money in a parking meter? Did you lend a dollar to a friend?

Progress Check 2

Write your answers on a separate piece of paper.

1. Make a list of all the things you spent money on in the last three days. Next to each one, write *N* if you needed the item. Write *W* if you wanted it but did not need it. As you start, your list will look something like this:

W	renting a video	$3.00
W	frozen yogurt	1.00
N	bus fare	8.00

2. When you finish, add up all the costs of things you needed in one column. Add up all the costs of things you wanted in another column. Compare the totals. How much did you spend on needs? On wants? What was the difference between the two?

Making an Expense Record

When you're on your own, your wants may change. But most of your needs will stay the same. You'll still need shelter, clothing, food, and transportation.

Jake has been living on his own for one month. He goes to community college at night, and he works during the day.

He shares an apartment with two friends. He has kept a record of his **expenses**, or what he spent, each week. He has a list for each week. Here are his lists.

Week 1		Week 2	
Magazine	$2.00	Dinner	$13.75
Lunch	4.25	Jeans	32.95
Groceries	26.00	Envelopes	1.29
Movie	5.50	Savings	25.00
Cleaning	11.25	Telephone	15.00
Gasoline	8.75	Groceries	16.00
Rent	250.00		
Books	41.29		

Week 3		Week 4	
Lunch	$3.50	Utilities	$12.00
Socks	3.50	Gasoline	17.50
Stamps	5.00	CD for brother's birthday	14.00
Groceries	15.00	Concert	15.00
Haircut	15.00	Parking	3.00
		Car **Insurance**	77.00
		Groceries	29.00

Progress Check 3

Use a separate piece of paper. Make a chart like the one shown on the facing page. Then use Jake's list of expenses to fill in the boxes on your chart. You will need to decide which expense fits each category. For example, gasoline is a transportation expense. Place the $8.75 Jake spent on gas next to *Transportation* under Week 1. Some items may not fit a category. Place these expenses in the row labeled *Other*.

Make sure you fill in the spaces for all four weeks. Include each of Jake's expenses.

Item	Week 1	Week 2	Week 3	Week 4	Total
Housing	—	—	—	—	—
Groceries	$26.00	$16.00	$15.00	$29.00	$86.00
Clothing	—	—	—	—	—
Transportation	—	—	—	—	—
Personal Care	—	—	—	—	—
Furniture	—	—	—	—	—
Recreation	—	—	—	—	—
Gifts	—	—	—	—	—
Utilities	—	—	—	—	—
Insurance	—	—	—	—	—
Loans	—	—	—	—	—
Books for School	—	—	—	—	—
Savings	—	—	—	—	—
Other	—	—	—	—	—
Total					

When your chart is done, use it to answer these questions.

1. How much did Jake spend for each category? Add across. Put the total in the last blank on the right of your chart. (*Groceries* has already been done for you. Copy the total on your chart. Then add the other totals.)
2. On what kind of expense did Jake spend the most money? On what did he spend the least?
3. Now add down. What were Jake's total expenses for Week 1? For Week 2? For Week 3? For Week 4?
4. What were Jake's total expenses for the whole month?

Income and Outgo

How does Jake get the money for all of his expenses? He makes it by working during the day at a service station. The money he makes is his **income**. The money he pays out for his expenses is often called **outgo**. When you add up all of your expenses, you know your outgo. (You figured your outgo for three days in Progress Check 2.)

When you are out on your own, your outgo should be less than your income. If it isn't, you will have to borrow money. For example, if you make $700 a month, your outgo can be $650, $600, or anything less than $700. You can't spend more than $700 without borrowing money.

Progress Check 4

Write your answers on a separate piece of paper.

1. You found out that your friend Philip's outgo was $692 last month. His income was $798. How much does he have left over?
2. Jill is working at Raffle's Bakery. Her income is $550 a month. Her outgo is $535. How much will she have left over?

What Are Variable and Fixed Expenses?

You can decide how much you want to spend on some things. For example, the amount that you spend on food and clothes is up to you. Expenses that you can control are called **variable** expenses. That means the amount is not always the same. It varies.

For example, one week you may spend $32 on groceries. The next week you may spend $29 or $15.

Solve It

$32 + $29 + $15 = Total amount spent on groceries for three weeks. How much is it?

Some of your expenses cannot be changed or controlled. These are called **fixed** expenses. They are the same each month. For example, every month your rent may be $250.

So your total outgo for each month is made up of two things. The first is variable expenses that you can control. The second is fixed expenses that you can't control.

Where Did Your Money Go in One Hour?

Imagine you're going out the door to work. It's 7:30 A.M. Your sister asks if she can borrow a dollar. You give it to her. You walk to the bus stop and take the same bus you take every day. You pay a dollar. The bus stops in front of the muffin shop. You go in and get two muffins and a cup of coffee. Your bill is $3.06. You walk a block to work. John is in charge of the office birthday fund. He explains that you need to pay $10 every year to the fund. You give him two five-dollar bills. It's now 8:30 A.M. How much did you spend in one hour? How much of it was fixed expenses? How much of it was variable?

Look at Martha's expense list on the next page. Decide which of the expenses are fixed and which are variable.

Martha's Monthly Expenses

apartment rent	$244.00	groceries	$43.36
birthday present	13.00	shirt	18.36
Burger Barn dinner	6.26	savings	15.00
car insurance	37.50	shoes	34.28
car payment	150.00	telephone	14.44
groceries	48.73	parking fees	8.50
groceries	31.00	movies	10.00
gasoline	43.96	car wax	12.52
utilities	32.00	snacks	10.90
haircut	15.00		

Progress Check 5

1. Fold a piece of paper in half lengthwise. On the left side of your paper, write *Fixed Expenses*. On the right side, write *Variable Expenses*. On your paper, list each of Martha's monthly expenses. Make sure to put each one in the correct column. Find the totals.

2. Martha's monthly income is $817.95. Add her fixed expenses and her variable expenses. Will Martha have any money left over from her monthly income? How much?

Monthly Income and Expenses

If you have a job, you know what you make each month. This is your monthly income. You also know what you must pay each month for rent and other fixed expenses. The difference between your income and fixed expenses shows what's left for variable expenses. In other words, you subtract your fixed expenses from your income. What's left is what you can save or spend on things you want.

Progress Check 6

Five jobs are listed below. Next to each job, an income is shown. So is an amount for fixed expenses. Number a separate sheet of paper from 1 to 5. For each job, subtract the fixed expense from the income. Write what is left for variable expenses.

Job	Income	Fixed Expenses	Variable Expenses
1. Security Guard	$750	$550	—
2. Stock Clerk	$658	$560	—
3. Fast Food Worker	$545	$467	—
4. Factory Worker	$820	$678	—
5. Counter Clerk	$529	$406	—

Calculator Practice

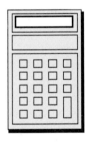

Try it on your calculator:

Enter 750

Then press the – key.

Then enter 550.

Press =

Your answer should be: $200

How Do You Buy Something You "Can't Afford"?

What do you do when you want to buy something big? There's no way you can pay for it from the money you have for variable expenses.

a.
$$\begin{array}{r} \$36.00 \\ \times 4 \\ \hline \end{array}$$

b.
$$\begin{array}{r} \$42.10 \\ \times 3 \\ \hline \end{array}$$

c.
$$3\overline{)\$39.00}$$

d.
$$6\overline{)\$148.00}$$

And you certainly can't pay for it from the money you have for fixed expenses.

You've been wanting a CD player exactly like the one your friend has. The player costs $350.

Progress Check 7

Write your answers on a separate piece of paper.

1. After you pay your fixed expenses, you have $237 left for variable expenses. You want the $350 CD player as soon as possible. How much would you have to save every month for 3 months to be able to buy the player? For 4 months? For 5 months?
2. Suppose you want a guitar. It costs $681. How much would you have to save every month for 6 months to be able to buy the guitar? For 7 months?
3. Let's say you saved $22 every month for 6 months. Would that be enough to buy a VCR that costs $200? If not, how much more would you need?

Do You Understand About Spending?

All this talk about money can be confusing. See how much you can remember about things like wants, needs, income, outgo, variable expenses, and fixed expenses.

Progress Check 8

Copy the numbers of these questions on a separate piece of paper. Read each statement. If the statement is true, write *T* next to the number on your paper. If the statement is false, write *F* next to the number.

1. Your wants and needs are always the same things.
2. Money you make is called outgo.
3. Money you pay for your expenses is called outgo.
4. Expenses you can control are called variable expenses.
5. Expenses you can't control are called fixed expenses.
6. You can pay for things that cost a lot if you plan ahead for the cost.

Math on the Job

Here's a Tip: Do you want something that costs a lot? Read the classified ads in the newspaper. You may get just what you want—and cheaper, too! Often, the owner needs cash or is moving.

Write your answers on a separate piece of paper.

1. Jerome has a job that requires a clean shirt every day. It costs $1.25 to have a shirt washed and ironed. What is Jerome's fixed expense for clean shirts in a five-day week?
2. If Marla takes the bus to work, she pays 50¢ a day. If she carpools, she pays 75¢ a day. How much does she save if she takes a bus for five days?
3. If Duane packs his lunch, it costs about $10.50 for a five-day week. If he uses the lunch wagon, it costs about $3.50 a day. How much does he save each week by packing a lunch?
4. Mark's fixed expenses to get to work include $1 a day for bus fare. He also pays $3 for lunch. How much does he need for bus fare and lunch for a five-day week?
5. Alice spent these amounts on lunch during a five-day week at work: $3.50, $4.50, $3.25, $5.50, and $4.25. What was her average expense for lunch? (Hint: Add, and divide the total by 5.)

Chapter Review

Chapter Summary

- It is important to tell the difference between things that you want and things that you need. When you're on your own, you'll spend money on both.

- You can find out where your money goes by keeping a personal expense record.

- A fixed expense does not usually change. You do not have any control over it.

- A variable expense is one you can control. It is not the same each month.

- The money you earn on your job is called income. The money you pay out for expenses is called outgo.

- You need to pay fixed expenses first. What you have left can be used for variable expenses.

- If you want something costly, you need to figure how much you must save each month to buy the item. Then you have a plan for buying it.

Chapter Quiz

You have seen how a personal expense record shows where money goes. This record shows you where Tracy's money went. Look at the record. Then answer the questions on a separate piece of paper.

housing	$250.00	gifts	$5.00
food	86.00	utilities	37.50
clothing	45.87	car insurance	90.00
transportation	34.00	car loan	100.00
personal care	24.50	savings	25.00
recreation	12.00		

1. What was Tracy's largest expense for the month? What was the smallest?
2. How much did she spend on recreation and gifts together?
3. How much more did she spend on food than clothing?
4. Her fixed expenses were housing, utilities, car insurance, and her car loan. What was the total of her fixed expenses?
5. What was the total of her variable expenses?
6. Which was more—her fixed or variable expenses?
7. Tracy's income is $744.83 a month. Is that enough to cover her total outgo?
8. If your income were $698.00, would you be able to afford the same expenses as Tracy? How much more would you need?

Challenge

Dan's income is $632 a month. Dan's friend Dave wants Dan to be his new roommate. Dan's part of the rent will be $287.50. Dan knows it is a good idea to pay rent that is no more than one-fourth of his income. Do you think Dan should move in with Dave? Explain the reason for your decision. (Helpful hint: To find one-fourth of a number, divide the number by 4.)

2 Making and Changing Your Budget

Careful budgeting helps you pay your bills and other expenses.

Chapter Learning Objectives

- Identify and predict spending and savings patterns.
- Prepare a budget of fixed and variable expenses.
- Compare ways to make your income meet your needs.
- List three steps you can take when a budget is overspent.
- List three ways to cope with financial emergencies.
- Review basic math skills in the Appendix at the back of this textbook.

Words to Know

budget   a plan for spending and saving money

balanced budget   a situation in which the total outgo matches income

budget item   a line with details about a particular expense or savings entry

debt   money that is owed

predict   to make a guess about the future

time payments   money paid, usually monthly, until the total bill is paid

transfer   to move money from one budget line to another

What Is a Budget?

A **budget** is a plan for what you're going to do with your income. Your budget is a list of expenses that you think you're going to have and money you want to save. A budget helps you to know if you can afford a CD at the end of the month, or to see a movie this week, or to go out for dinner tonight.

What's In a Budget?

A budget has three main parts. The first part is made up of fixed expenses. These are the bills you have to pay every month.

The second part is the amount you want to save every month. You save for things that cost a lot, such as cars and TV sets.

The third part of your budget is made up of variable expenses.

Savings and variable expenses are the parts of your budget that you can change. You can't change fixed expenses.

Why Should a Budget Be Balanced?

Setting up a budget takes a little work. But it will make your life easier in the long run.

Suppose you're working at a chewing gum factory. You live in an apartment with your roommate, who works in a restaurant. Your income is $725 a month. You and your roommate split the cost of rent, phone, utilities, and cable TV.

Solve It

Here are the costs you and your roommate split:

rent	$400
phone	16
utilities	20
cable TV	16

If you had to pay them all yourself, how much would you need?

You're saving money to go to computer night school. You cook for yourself most of the time. You also go out on dates.

To do all these things, you must have a **balanced budget**. You can't spend and save more than your total income without going into **debt**.

Look at the monthly budget below. Read each **budget item**. Remember that there are four weeks in an average month. So weekly expenses, such as groceries, are multiplied by four.

Your Monthly Budget

Income:		$725.00
Fixed Expenses:	Rent (your half)	200.00
	Gas and electricity (your half)	10.00
	Phone (your half)	8.00
	Cable TV (your half)	8.00
Savings:	For computer night school	75.00
	For gifts and emergencies	10.00
Variable Expenses:	Groceries ($35 per week x 4 weeks)	140.00
	Laundry ($4.50 per week x 4 weeks)	18.00
	Transportation (bus fare)	56.00
	Clothing	25.00
	Drugstore, personal care	16.00
	Haircut	15.00
	Recreation ($36.00 per week x 4 weeks)	144.00
	Total Expenses:	$725.00

Progress Check 1

Use the above budget to answer these questions. Write your answers on a separate piece of paper.

1. How much money are you saving every month?
2. How much money will you have saved for computer night school after 12 months?
3. A round trip on the bus (going there and coming back) costs $2.00. How many round trips does the transportation budget pay for in a month?

What If Your Budget Is Wrong?

In making your budget, you forget some things. Most people do, the first time.

You forget that you'll need steel-toed boots for your new job in the factory. You'll also need special pants and shirts because it's greasy work. The new work clothes will cost $60. You can use **time payments** for six months at the clothing store. If you divide $60 by 6, you get $10. So you need to add $10 (plus interest) to your monthly clothing budget. Then you can get the clothes you need now. You already had $25 in your budget. So you add $10 and get $35.

Also, you'll need a special wash load every week for the greasy work clothes. That adds $5 a month to your laundry cost.

Then there's the cat that you and your roommate decide to take in. You didn't know cat food and cat litter cost so much. Your half of that expense is $2.75 a week. That adds $11 a month to your grocery bill.

Did You Know?
The expense budget for the U.S.A. in 1990 was $1,151,800,000,000.00. That's one trillion, one-hundred-and-fifty-one billion, eight-hundred million dollars. And it's not balanced!

How Can You Pay for These Extra Costs?

You won't get a pay raise until next year. So you have to change your budget plan. You have to balance expenses and income. You do this by subtracting money from savings and variable expenses. Then you **transfer** the money you subtract to cover the added expenses. The hard part is choosing which variable expenses to give up or reduce.

Which Budget Items Can You Change?

If you transfer money from school savings, you'll wait longer to get your special training. If you take away from personal care, you won't look the way you want to look. If you subtract bus rides, you'll have to walk or stay home. Cut into gifts and Mom's birthday present may disappear.

Progress Check 2

Write your answers on a separate piece of paper. Base your answers on this chart:

Savings for computer night school	$75.00
Savings for gifts and emergencies	10.00
Bus fare	56.00
Drugstore, personal care	16.00
Recreation	144.00

1. You need to add $10 to clothing, $5 to laundry, and $11 to groceries. What is the total of these new expenses?
2. Subtract the total of the new expenses from recreation. How much is left for recreation?
3. Your first budget gave you $36 a week for 4 weeks of recreation. What is the new weekly total?

Should You Start Night School Now or Wait?

You've saved for a year to pay for computer school. You have $900 in the bank. Now the computer school is offering just the right night course for you.

A new friend at work is also going to take the course. Lucky for you, the friend has a car! He will drive you to work with him and also to your home after school. He'll charge just $6.50 a week for gas money.

But the course costs $1,200. And you'll have to buy a $700 personal computer to do homework. That adds up to $1,900. If you borrow $1,000 from a finance company, the finance charge will be big.

But most of these new expenses are matched by budget cuts. You won't have a monthly savings for school. And paying $6.50 a week for riding with your friend will be much cheaper than riding the bus.

Look at the Budget Changes for Night School chart. It shows how going to night school will change your budget.

Budget Changes for Night School

Amounts Added to Your Budget	Amounts Subtracted from Your Budget
• Your loan for a year from the finance company will cost $116 a month.	• $75 per month for savings for night school will be subtracted.
• Monthly gas money to your friend will add $26.	• $48 for bus fare round trips will be subtracted.

This is one reason a budget is important. Your budget helps you figure out the best way to use your income. You can compare added costs and subtracted costs. Then it's clear that you can afford to take the night computer course.

And the computer training will help you get jobs that pay more than your present job.

Progress Check 3

Write your answers on a separate piece of paper. Base your answers on the Budget Changes for Night School chart.

1. What is the total added monthly cost of taking the night school course?
2. How much can you subtract from your budget because of night school?
3. Which is bigger, the costs you'll add, or the costs you'll subtract? How much bigger?
4. Look at the answer to question 3. This is the amount you have to transfer from some other variable expense to balance the budget. It's not a lot. In fact, you can do it by giving up something small—like a late-night pizza. At $9.50 each, how many pizzas per month would you have to give up?
5. You'll pay $116 a month to the finance company. How much will you pay in 12 months?

They're Not All the Same: Finance companies charge high rates for small loans. But finance companies are the only places where some people can get small loans. Compare rates before you borrow.

How Does the Budget Look Now?

You've made a lot of changes in your budget. Here is what it looks like now:

Your Changed Monthly Budget

Income:		$725.00
Fixed Expenses:	Rent (your half)	$200.00
	Gas and Electricity (your half)	10.00
	Phone (your half)	8.00
	Cable TV (your half)	8.00
	Loan payment	116.00

(continued on next page)

Your Changed Monthly Budget (continued)

Savings:	For gifts and emergencies	10.00
Variable Expenses:	Groceries $35 per week x 4 weeks	140.00
	Laundry $5.75 per week x 4 weeks	23.00
	Clothing	35.00
	Transportation (gas money)	26.00
	Drugstore, personal care	16.00
	Haircut	15.00
	Recreation ($29.50 per week x 4 weeks)	118.00
	Total Expenses	$725.00

What About Changes You Can't Predict?

Here's a Tip: Making a budget is easier than sticking to it. Don't be surprised if you have some trouble at first. You'll get better at it!

Something has happened that you couldn't **predict**. Your landlord is selling the apartment building you're living in. You'll have to move. And your roommate has decided to go to work on his grandfather's ranch for a year. You're going to have to get a new place on your own.

You find a place you like for $300 a month. But now you have to pay the total of the rent, gas, electricity, cable TV, and phone. The utilities bills aren't as high as they were with two people. But they're more than you've been paying. And your cost for cable TV has doubled.

You get a 20¢ per hour raise at work. But that's not enough. So you get an extra job. You take two four-hour evening shifts at Mammoth Burger.

Here's how you balance your new budget.

Budget Increases

Increased Monthly Income	Increased Monthly Expenses
• Hourly raise at work yields monthly increase of $25 after taxes. • Eight evening hours weekly at Mammoth Burger add $87 a month after taxes.	• Rent up $100. • Gas and electricity up $7. • Phone up $8. • Cable TV up $8.

Basics Practice

a.
```
    16
  x  6
```

b.
```
4)473.48
```

c.
```
    47
    31
    28
  + 14
```

Progress Check 4

Use the Budget Increases chart to answer these questions. Write your answers on a separate piece of paper.

1. How much is the total increase in monthly income?
2. How much is the total increase in monthly expenses?
3. Which is larger, expenses or income? How much larger?
4. You were paying half of the cable TV bill. Alone, it costs you $16 a month. If you drop cable TV, will that cover the remainder of the added expense? How much will be left over to put into recreation?

What Happens in Emergencies?

What happens to your budget when emergencies come up? This was your unlucky week!

Your home computer broke, and you had to take it in for repairs.

The computer store said it would cost $160 to fix it! They said you'd have to pay the whole bill to get the computer back.

Next, you left your wallet on the counter in Jim's Diner. When you went back, it was gone. You lost your wallet and $30.

Then you sprained your wrist playing basketball on Sunday. You went to the emergency room. The doctors took X-rays and put you in a splint. The bill was $140. It wasn't covered by the factory's health insurance plan. So far, how much extra did this week cost you, not counting the price of a new wallet?

Calculator Practice

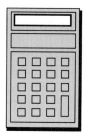

Enter 160

Press +

Enter 30

Press +

Enter 140

Press =

Your answer should be: $330

Wordwise: When you cut back on your spending, you *scrimp*. The word comes from the Swedish word *skrympa*, which means *to shrink.*

For five days, you couldn't work. You had already used your sick leave. So you lost a week's pay! You also missed two night shifts at Mammoth Burger. You cut back on your spending. But you'll still be short at the end of the month.

The finance company lets you put off your loan payment for one month. But your monthly budget is still short. And you have $300 in unpaid bills. What will you do?

Should You Borrow Money?

Your emergency savings cover part of the need. You decide you can't afford to borrow more money. You would prefer to pay off your debts a little at a time. So you will do it month by month. You combine money from your clothing, recreation, and savings budget into a monthly repayment fund.

Monthly Repayment Fund

Transferred from clothing	$20 a month
Transferred from recreation	20 a month
Transferred from gifts and emergencies	10 a month
Total	$50 a month

The monthly repayment fund now becomes a fixed expense. That is because you need to make the same payment each month to get out of debt.

You call the hospital and the computer store. You explain your emergency. You tell them you'll be able to pay your debts in six monthly payments. They're not happy, but they accept the deal.

Progress Check 5

Write your answers on a separate piece of paper. Base your answers on the Monthly Repayment Fund chart.

1. What is the total monthly repayment fund?
2. In six months, the repayment fund will exactly pay your debts. How much money do you owe?

A Different Problem: Budgeting Extra Money

Imagine that you've paid off your debts. After all your bad luck, there's some good news. You're being promoted. You'll be an assistant to the foreman. Your pay is now $7.50 an hour. That adds $225 a month to your budget.

Your friends have lots of suggestions for you. Buy some camping equipment! Buy a CD player! Get a microwave oven!

But first, you want to quit working at Mammoth Burger. You had switched to working 8 hours each Saturday because of night school. Quitting your Saturday job will subtract $87 a month from your total income.

Here is the way you figure out what you will have after you quit Mammoth Burger.

Changes in Your Income

Your income on the old budget	Add your 20¢ raise plus two shifts at Mammoth Burger	Add $225 from your promotion	Subtract your $87 job at Mammoth Burger to get	Your new income
$725	$837	$1,062	$975	$975

Solve It

After you quit your job at Mammoth Burger, what will your new income be? How much more is that than your income on your old budget?

What Can You Do with Your Extra Money?

You use time payments to buy a car and a new TV! You decide to start buying clothes again at $35 a month. You're not doing greasy work anymore. You're also going to get cable TV again, and you will save for gifts and emergencies. You'll also give yourself a little more for recreation. But most of the raise goes into monthly repayment.

Here is your budget with your new income:

Your Newly Adjusted Monthly Budget

Income:		$975.00
Fixed Expenses:	Rent	$300.00
	Gas and Electricity	15.00
	Phone	15.00
	Cable TV	16.00
	Time payments for car and TV	228.00
Savings:	For gifts and emergencies	10.00
Variable Expenses:	Groceries ($36.25 per week x 4 weeks)	145.00
	Laundry ($4.50 per week x 4 weeks)	18.00
	Clothing	35.00
	Drugstore, personal care	14.00
	Haircut	15.00
	Recreation and casual expenses ($41 per week x 4 weeks)	164.00
	Total Expenses	$975.00

Progress Check 6

Use Your Newly Adjusted Monthly Budget chart to answer these questions. Write your answers on a separate piece of paper.

1. Your clothing budget was $15. How much more will you have for clothes now?

2. Your cable TV budget was $0. What is it now?

3. Your recreation budget was $118. How much can you spend now?

4. What's the difference between what you can spend now for recreation and what you could spend before?

5. If you budget $164 for recreation over a four-week month, how much is that a week?

6. What if you make some long-distance phone calls? Then you get the phone bill. It's $32.50. How much did you budget for the phone bill? How much will you need to transfer from variable expenses to pay for the extra phone charges?

7. From which variable expense would you transfer the money needed for the extra phone charges?

8. Your monthly grocery budget was $140. It is now $145. How much of a weekly increase is this?

9. Your original budget had a total of $373 for variable expenses. Your newly adjusted monthly budget has a total of how much for variable expenses? What's the difference between the two budgets?

Math on the Job

1. Scott's budget allows $15 per week for lunch. How much can he spend each day during a 5-day work week?

2. Felix will need $672 in 6 months for a class that will help him get a promotion. How much should he save each month?

3. Of the $672 Felix will need, $122 is for books, supplies, and transportation. How much is for tuition?

4. Sylvia pays $20 a month to have her uniforms cleaned. How much does this cost in 6 months?

5. Cliff has just lost his carpool driver. He now has to take the bus for an extra cost of $5.50 a week. How much is that per day, if Cliff works 5 days a week?

6. Anna's rent has gone up $10 a month, but her income is the same. She must cut into variable expenses to balance her budget.

   a. How many $2.00 bus trips would she have to give up to cover the increase?

   b. How many $1.00 frozen yogurts would pay for the increase?

   c. How many $5.00 movies would she have to miss?

   d. Find a combination of movies, bus trips, and frozen yogurts that totals $10.

Chapter Review

Chapter Summary

- A budget is a plan that shows how you're going to use your income.

- The three main parts of a budget are fixed expenses, variable expenses, and savings.

- Some variable expenses can be cut back to pay for changes in necessary expenses.

- Like variable expenses, savings can change from month to month.

- A budget helps you make choices about what to spend and what to save.

- A budget should always be balanced. That means total expenses and savings are equal to total income.

- A change in income or expenses may unbalance a budget. Adjusting the budget brings it back in balance.

- Emergencies can cause big, temporary increases in expenses.

- Borrowing money to pay for emergency budget increases can be very expensive.

- Borrowing money costs money. Repaying debt should have high priority in a personal budget.

Chapter Quiz

Write your answers on a separate sheet of paper.

Your Basic Monthly Budget

Rent	$200	Food	$120
Gas and electricity	15	Clothing	25
Telephone	15	Transportation	62
Loan payments	90	Personal care	29
Savings	75	Recreation	116

1. What is the total of this budget?

2. How much income is needed to balance the budget?

3. You owe $540 in loans. According to this budget, how long will it take to pay it back?

4. There are four weeks in the month. How much weekly money is there for recreation?

5. If you buy two $12 T-shirts this month, will you spend more or less than your budget allows?

6. How much money will you save in a year?

7. A monthly loan payment of $25 has been made. What is the new loan payment total for the month?

8. How much rent do you pay in a year?

9. A friend's monthly telephone, gas, and electricity bills come to $23. How much more do you pay?

10. Which costs more, recreation or food? How much more?

Challenge

Make a list of some variable expenses that you have every month. Be sure to write down the cost of each expense. Then decide which ones you could do without to save $25 a month.

Unit One Review

Read the sentences below. On a separate piece of paper, write a *T* next to the number of the sentence if the sentence is true. Write an *F* next to the number of the sentence if the sentence is false. Then rewrite the sentence to make it true.

1. Your income is the money you spend each month.

2. You cannot choose how much you want to spend on fixed expenses.

3. If your fixed expenses are high, you will have less money for variable expenses.

4. A budget helps you figure what you can afford to buy.

5. If your income falls or your expenses rise, you can cut back on your fixed expenses.

6. In a budget, income is balanced against savings and expenses.

7. A plan for saving and spending your money is called an income.

8. You cannot save money if you are on a budget.

9. Some bills, like rent and electricity, must be paid each month.

10. To balance your budget, you might need to cut back on the amount you spend for clothes.

Unit Two

Earning a Paycheck

3 Your Salary

Punching a timeclock keeps an exact record of how many hours you work each day.

Chapter Learning Objectives

- Figure a weekly, monthly, and yearly salary based on the number of hours worked and the hourly wage.
- Compare salaries for different occupations.
- Interpret a time card and figure the number of hours worked.
- Calculate overtime pay using the 1.5 and 2.0 overtime rates.
- Figure a salary based on an hourly wage plus tips.
- Review basic math skills in the Appendix at the back of this textbook.

Words to Know

application   form used to ask for something

employee   a person who works for another person or business for pay

employment   work; what a person does to earn a living

employment agency   a company that, for a fee, helps people find jobs

hourly   every 60 minutes

monthly   each month

overtime   beyond regular hours

salary   fixed pay for regular work

time card   a paper or card on which hours worked by an employee are recorded

wage   amount paid for work

weekly   every seven days

How Do You Look for a Job?

There may be a time that you will want to try another kind of job. Perhaps the company you're working for has to let some **employees** go. Or perhaps you just get tired of your job. In either case, you'll need to start thinking about how to find something better.

There are several ways to find a new job when you want or need one. Here are five ways:

1. Put in an **application** at the place where you want to work.
2. Talk to your school placement service.

3. Talk to friends who work where you want to work. Ask them to let you know when any jobs open up.

4. Go to an **employment agency**.

5. Read the **employment** ads in the paper.

How Do You Figure the Yearly Salary from an Ad?

Take a look at this ad. It is for a counter person in an ice cream store.

COUNTER PERSON for Scotts Valley ice cream store. Courteous & reliable applicant for evening shift. Must be at least 18. $5–$5.25 hr. to start. Apply in person, 582 Mt. Hermon Rd. 555-5578

Suppose this job sounds interesting to you. You want to find out what the yearly **salary** is. You see that the job pays $5.25 **hourly** to start. But the ad doesn't tell you the number of hours you would work. You call and find out that the job is for 40 hours a week. Now you can figure out the yearly income.

Did You Know?
Employment agencies will tell you about jobs that are open. Usually you have to pay a fee to get the names of the places that need workers.

First, figure out how much you'll make in a week:

$5.25 an hour x 40 hours a week = $210 a week.

Second, figure out how much you'll make in an average month of four weeks:

$210 a week x 4 weeks = $840.

Third, figure out about how much you'll make a year:

$840 a month x 12 months = $10,080 a year.

Fourth, figure out how much you'll make in a year if you get a paid vacation:

$210 a week x 52 weeks = $10,920 a year.

Here are four employment ads from the newspaper. Read each one. You'll see that each one has a different **weekly** salary.

PLUMBERS, $10–$20 hr. + medical. Exp. in resident & comm. 555-7228.

CARPENTERS - apprentice to journey level. $8–$16. hr. + medical. 555-4749.

DRIVER needed for hauling service. Must have phone, own transportation & current DMV printout. $5 hr. to start. $6 after 30 days with chance of advancement & more money. Call 555-5777.

NURSING
  RN $15/hr.
  LVN $13/hr.
needed for long-term care facility. New hire bonus – 1 week vacation after 6 months.
Call Peggy, 555-8832

Basics Practice

a. $5.25
    x .40

b. $350.90
    – 290.85

c. $22.40
    x .40

d. $600.29
    – 450.17

Progress Check 1

Write your answers on a separate piece of paper.

1. How much will the driver job pay after 30 days? What will it pay for a 40-hour week after 30 days? (40 x $6 = ?) What will it pay for a 4-week month? (4 x weekly pay = ?)

2. How much will the driver job pay for the first week? (40 x $5 = ?) How much more could you make in the seventh week than in the first? (Seventh week's pay – first week's pay = ?)

3. An RN is a registered nurse. An LVN is a licensed vocational nurse. What is the hourly pay for an LVN? How much more will the RN make in a week than the LVN?

4. Who could make more at top pay—the carpenter or the plumber? How much more for a 40-hour week?

What Is the Salary on the Job?

Here are some jobs that many people like doing. See if any of them sound interesting to you.

Job	Yearly Salary	Monthly Salary	Weekly Salary
Bank teller	$12,000	—	—
Painter	23,520	—	—
Dental assistant	12,480	—	—
Welder	28,992	—	—
Sheet metal worker	37,008	—	—
Telephone operator	19,680	—	—
Police officer	24,576	—	—
Bus driver	21,024	—	—

The first column shows the salary for the year. To find out a **monthly** salary, divide the yearly salary by 12 months.

$12,000 yearly salary ÷ 12 months

= $1,000 a month

To find out a **weekly** salary, divide the yearly salary by 52 weeks.

Calculator Practice

Enter 12000

Press ÷

Enter 52

Press =

Your answer should be: 230.76923 or $230.77

Progress Check 2

Use the yearly salary on the chart to figure the monthly and weekly salary for each job. Next, write your answers for the questions below on a separate sheet of paper.

1. Who makes more—the dental assistant or the bank teller? ($12,480 – $12,000 = ?) How much more?
2. Who makes more—the welder or the sheet metal worker? ($37,008 – $28,992 = ?) How much more?
3. Who makes more—the painter or the police officer? How much more?
4. Suppose the telephone operator didn't get a raise for two years. What would this person earn from the job in two years?
5. If a police officer were married to a bank teller, what would their combined incomes be each month?
6. If a bus driver were married to a telephone operator, what would their combined incomes be each month?
7. Which job on the list would you most like to have? Tell why.
8. Which job on the list would you least like to have? Tell why.

Rounding Dollars and Cents: Look at the third number after the decimal. If it's 5 or higher, round up. If it's 4 or lower, round down. (Examples: 1.56\underline{7}$ = $1.57 and 1.56\underline{4}$ = $1.56.)

How Do You Fill Out a Time Card?

The place where you work may ask you to use a **time card**. A clerk may write down your hours on the card. Or you may need to put your card into a special clock that stamps the time when you stop work.

Look at this listing from a time card. It shows the date. It also shows the hour you started work and the hour you stopped work. Your lunch time is listed as one hour.

Time Card

Name: Mike Quinn   Job Title: Assembler

Hourly Rate: $7   Week Ending: 6/16

Day	Date	Time In	Time Out	Lunch Time	Total Hours
Monday	6/12	4 P.M.	12 P.M.	1 hour	7 hours

How Do You Figure Your Hours?

Suppose the hours you worked were from 4 P.M. until midnight. How many hours did you work? Find your hours this way:

$$\begin{array}{r} 12 \text{ P.M.} \\ - \ 4 \text{ P.M.} \\ \hline \end{array}$$
8 hours – 1 hour for lunch = 7 hours worked

Wordwise: A.M. stands for the hours between midnight and noon. P.M. refers to the hours from noon to midnight.

Sometimes you will need to subtract A.M. hours from P.M. hours or P.M. hours from A.M. hours. Then you'll add 12 to the smaller number before you subtract from it.

Today you worked from 7 A.M. until 4 P.M. You took off one hour for lunch. This is to find out how many hours you worked:

$$\begin{array}{r} 4{:}00 \text{ P.M.} \ + 12 \\ - \ 7{:}00 \text{ A.M.} \\ \hline \end{array} = \begin{array}{r} 16{:}00 \\ - \ 7{:}00 \\ \hline \end{array}$$
9:00 – 1 hour for lunch
= 8 hours worked

Solve It

Find the number of hours worked for the times below. (Subtract 1 hour for lunch each time.)

1. From 8 A.M. to 5 P.M.
2. From 11 P.M. to 7 A.M.

If you work at a cannery, your hours may not always be the same. Sometimes you go to work in the morning. Sometimes you need to work in the afternoon or at night. Here's a cannery worker's time card for one week.

Day	Date	Time In	Time Out	Lunch Time	Total Hours
Monday	6/12	4 P.M.	12 midnight	1 hour	7 hours
Tuesday	6/13	7 A.M.	4 P.M.	1 hour	—
Wednesday	6/14	12 midnight	7 A.M.	1 hour	—
Thursday	6/15	4 P.M.	12 midnight	1 hour	—
Friday	6/16	7 A.M.	4 P.M.	1 hour	—

Progress Check 3

On a separate piece of paper, figure the hours this person worked for each day. Then add them. How many hours did this person work this week?

How Do You Figure Overtime?

Sometimes you may work **overtime** on your job. This means you work longer than the amount of time you are scheduled to work.

You're supposed to work 40 hours a week. This week you worked 45 hours. That is 5 hours overtime.

Here is the way you would find how many hours of overtime you worked.

45 hours of time actually worked
– 40 hours you were scheduled to work
5 hours overtime

When you work overtime in some jobs, you get paid more than your regular hourly **wage**. Suppose your wage is $6 an hour. If you work overtime, you get one and one-half times your hourly wage. Here's how to figure your overtime pay: Multiply 1.5 by $6.00.

Basics Practice

a.
```
    58
 –  40
```

b.
```
   1.5
 x   5
```

c.
```
  $5.75
 x  1.5
```

d.
```
  $4.25
 x    2
```

Calculator Practice

Try it on your calculator:

Enter 1.5.

Then press the x key

then enter 6.

Press =

Your answer should be: $9

If your regular wage is $6 an hour, your overtime wage is $9 an hour. How much would you make for working 5 hours of overtime?

To find out, multiply the number of hours you worked overtime by your hourly overtime wage.

$ 9 hourly overtime wage
x   5 hours of overtime
$45

You would make $45 by working 5 hours of overtime. So far, you have $45 extra dollars for this month. If you get another 5 hours of overtime next week, you'd have $90 extra!

Progress Check 4

Here's a Tip: When you're paid twice your normal hourly rate, it's called "doubletime." Many jobs pay doubletime for work on Christmas Day, Thanksgiving, and other holidays.

Write your answers on a separate piece of paper.

1. Michelle's regular hourly wage at the candy factory is $7. Her overtime rate is double. This means two times her regular hourly wage. Find out what she gets for one hour of overtime. (2 x $7 = ?) What would she get for 10 hours of overtime?

2. Isaac is working as a security guard. What would his overtime pay be if his usual hourly rate is $6.75 and his overtime rate is double? (2 x $6.75 = ?)

3. Ariel is working at a meat-packing plant. Her regular wage is $8 an hour. Her overtime rate is one and a half times her usual wage. (1.5 x $8 = ?) This week she worked 3 hours of overtime each night. (3 hours x overtime wage = overtime pay each night) What will Ariel get paid for 5 nights' overtime?

How Do You Figure Your Income When You Make Tips?

Some jobs involve giving service to people. You may enjoy being around people and providing services to others. If so, you might like one of these jobs:

waiter	taxi driver	hotel doorman
waitress	skycap	hotel bellhop

All the people with jobs like these receive tips for their services.

When you give a waiter or a taxi driver a tip, it's a way to tell the person you liked his or her service.

Darryl is the doorman at the Insideout Inn. He calls taxis for people. He opens doors. He helps with packages. He gives directions. He watches to see if there is anything he can do for visitors. Today, all in one hour, a man gave him $5 for getting a cab during rush hour. Then a woman tipped him $2 for carrying a big box inside the hotel. Next, a man asked Darryl to watch some packages while he ran back to his room. He tipped Darryl $1. So in one hour, Darryl earned $8 in tips.

Wordwise: A skycap is an employee who carries passenger baggage at an airport. A bellhop does the same for people staying at a hotel.

How do you figure your income plus tips for a week? Each week you work 30 hours at your job. You get paid $4.25 an hour. In four weeks you make $510. But you also make around $275 a week in tips. In four weeks that means you make $1,100 in tips. (4 x $275 = $1,100)

Progress Check 5

Number a separate piece of paper from 1 to 5. Write the total weekly salary for each employee listed.

Employee	Hourly Wage	Hours Worked	Tips for the Week	Weekly Income
1. Todd (waiter)	$4.25	30	$450	—
2. Sal (skycap)	$3.75	40	$200	—
3. Gene (cafe musician)	$4.50	15	$75	—
4. Cindy (hotel maid)	$3.60	35	$50	—
5. Jan (cafe hostess)	$6.25	20	$100	—

What About Expenses on the Job?

You may have a job that requires you to wear a uniform. If so, you will need to buy or rent the uniform. You'll also need to have it cleaned and pressed for work. This can cost extra money. It's money that takes away from money that you earn.

For example, if you're a deputy sheriff, your uniforms will cost about $340. Cleaning costs will be about $320 a year. You have two shirts and one pair of pants dry-cleaned every week. Here is how it makes a difference in your salary.

Deputy sheriff's salary	Uniform cost per year	Income after buying uniforms	Cleaning bill for a year	Income after buying uniforms and having them cleaned
$28,000	− $340	= $27,660	− $320	= $27,340

Progress Check 6

Write your answers on a separate piece of paper.

1. Bob is a carpenter. He needs to buy these tools for work:

framing hammer	$22
four-foot level	$18
carpenter's square	$ 7

   What are his total expenses for tools?

2. Bob's salary is $486 a week. He gets a two-week paid vacation. What is Bob's yearly salary? (Hint: There are 52 weeks in a year.)

3. What is Bob's yearly income after buying his tools?

Math on the Job

Write your answers on a separate piece of paper.

1. Larry Vargas drives a cab for the Move It Taxicab Company. The company charges Larry 50% of his earnings for use of the cab. Last week Larry took in $580 in fares. How much did he have after he paid Move It 50%?

2. Leroy Johnson is a house painter who has just been paid for a job. Leroy's check for $960 includes the $85 he paid for paint. What does Leroy make after subtracting the price of the paint from his check?

3. Jerry Lau is a skycap at the airport. His weekly salary is $175. Last week Jerry made $129 in tips. When Jerry figured his total income for the week, he added his tips to his wages. What did he make in that week?

4. Belinda Schwartz is the payroll clerk at the Fantasy Furniture Co. This week the senior salesperson earned $430. The other two salespeople earned $357 each. How much does Belinda put on the salesroom payroll?

5. Celia Ruiz is the timekeeper at the Spinaca Cannery. This week, 66 workers each put in 5 hours of overtime. Celia needs to put all of the overtime hours onto the payroll. How many hours of overtime will there be?

6. Each of the workers at Spinaca Cannery earns $4.25 an hour. They get one and one-half times their hourly rate for each overtime hour. How much does one worker make for 1 hour of overtime? How much is made for 5 hours of overtime?

7. Since 66 workers each put in 5 hours of overtime, how much must Spinaca Cannery pay just in overtime hours?

8. Roberto Luis was happy about the overtime hours at the cannery. He worked 40 hours at his regular $4.25 rate plus 5 extra hours at the overtime rate. What will be his total wages for the week?

9. Roberto is hoping he can get the overtime hours each week. If he gets the same hours each week, how much will he earn for the month (4 weeks)?

10. There are 250 employees at the Spinaca Cannery. 200 of the employees each put in 5 hours overtime. Each employee has a regular rate of $4.25. How much in overtime will the cannery pay?

Chapter Review

Chapter Summary

- There are several good ways to find a new job. One way is to read the classified employment ads in the newspaper.

- You can figure a weekly salary by multiplying your hourly wage by the number of hours you work a week.

- You can figure a four-week (about a month) salary by multiplying your weekly wages by four weeks.

- You can figure a yearly salary by multiplying your weekly wages by 52 weeks.

- You can find your monthly income by dividing your yearly income by 12.

- You can find your weekly income by dividing your yearly income by 52.

- At some jobs you will use a time card. Sometimes a clerk marks your work hours on the card. Sometimes a timeclock prints the time you start work and the time you stop.

- To figure the number of hours you work in a day, subtract the hour you began from the hour you stopped. Then subtract the time you took for lunch.

- Overtime is the amount of time you work beyond the time you're scheduled to work. The hourly rate for overtime is often 1.5 times your regular hourly wage. Sometimes it is double your regular hourly wage.

- To find your overtime pay, multiply the number of hours you worked overtime by your overtime wage.

- Some service jobs pay a salary and tips. When you figure your income, add the salary and the tips.

- Sometimes a job has expenses for tools or uniforms. These costs lower the amount you actually make on the job.

Chapter Quiz

Write your answers on a separate sheet of paper.

1. Velma read about a job in the paper. It's a job in a cabinet shop. The job pays $5 an hour. If she gets the job, Velma would work a 40-hour week. How much would she make in four weeks?

2. Ralph's working as a stock person for $4.75 an hour. He works 35 hours a week. What will he make in four weeks?

3. If Gabe's yearly salary as a bus driver is $21,000, how much will he make in one month?

4. Figure how many hours May worked if she started work at 9 A.M. and stopped work at 2 P.M.

5. Amy worked overtime for 8 hours last week. Her regular hourly wage is $5.50. Her overtime rate is one and one-half, or 1.5. What is her overtime hourly wage?

6. Nguyen had been a waiter at Steve's Silver Spoon for one night. His first night he made $40 in tips. His hourly wage is $7 an hour. He worked from 6 P.M. until 11 P.M. What did he make his first night?

7. Emma works as a taxi driver. She gets a wage of $240 a week. She makes $40 a night in tips. She works 7 nights a week. How much does she make in one week?

8. Rosemary has to buy a uniform for her job at the hospital. The uniform costs $45. She buys four uniforms a year. What will she spend in one year on uniforms? If her salary is $24,000, what does she have left after buying uniforms?

Challenge

Write a list of the four jobs you would most like to have. Next to each job, tell why you would like to have it. Find out the salary for the job. (You can find out average salaries at the library. Or you can ask someone you know who works the job.) Compare the jobs you like with those of other people in your class. Does anyone else have the same list as yours?

4 Your Take-home Pay

Your paycheck stub shows the difference between your salary and your take-home pay.

Chapter Learning Objectives

- Identify some common deductions that may be subtracted from earnings.
- Determine net pay by subtracting total deductions from gross pay.
- Compare various employees' salaries and deductions.
- Interpret an earnings statement.
- Interpret a pie chart and a bar graph.
- Review basic math skills in the Appendix at the back of this textbook.

Words to Know

allowance a reduction in your tax for each person you support, including yourself

deduction an amount subtracted from gross pay for a tax, a benefit, a service, or a membership

earnings statement the check stub attached to your paycheck listing gross pay, deductions, and net pay

gross pay amount of salary earned

net pay amount of salary received after deductions have been taken

tax money paid to the national treasury or the state treasury

withheld kept out

What Does Gross Pay Mean?

The salary you earn is called your **gross pay**. Your take-home pay is called your **net pay**. Gross pay is what you earn before deductions. Your net pay is what you earn after deductions. So what is a deduction?

Kinds of Deductions

A **deduction** is an amount of money **withheld** from your paycheck to pay for something else. A deduction can pay for a **tax**, a benefit, a service, or a membership. Some common deductions are listed on the next page.

They're Not All the Same: Low incomes are taxed at a lower rate than high incomes.

- **Federal Income Tax**   the money you pay from your salary to the treasury of the United States
- **Social Security (FICA)**   a plan that makes support payments to older people
- **State Tax**   the money you pay from your salary to the treasury of your state
- **Health Insurance**   a plan that helps pay your medical bills
- **Disability Insurance**   a plan that pays employees who can't work because they are injured or sick
- **United Fund**   a sum of money that you choose to give to organizations that help people
- **Union Dues**   money paid by members of organizations that help workers get what they need from employers
- **Credit Union**   a savings and loan business that serves company employees

There may be other deductions from your salary. The place where you work will have its own list of deductions. Those listed above are the deductions that are most often taken from paychecks. In fact, two of them are taken from almost every paycheck. They are the first two listed—Federal Income Tax and Social Security (FICA).

What Are Federal Income Tax and FICA?

The federal income tax deduction is not the same for every person. Yours may be different from someone else's. It depends on the amount you earn. It also depends on how many **allowances** you claim on your taxes. A tax allowance is usually the number of people you support. For example, if you support yourself, you can claim one allowance. That means you depend on yourself for support.

Wordwise: FICA stands for Federal Insurance Contribution Act. It is a form of insurance set up by our government in 1935 to protect people against loss of income. Usually we call it Social Security.

The Social Security tax or FICA you pay is a percentage of your salary. The FICA rate can change from time to time.

Progress Check 1

Write the letters of your answers on a separate piece of paper.

1. What is gross pay?
   a. your full salary before deductions
   b. your salary after deductions
   c. money received for tips

2. What is money you pay from your salary to the treasury of the U.S.?
   a. state income tax
   b. federal income tax
   c. United Fund

3. What is FICA?
   a. union dues
   b. medical insurance
   c. Social Security

4. What is a deduction?
   a. money added to your salary
   b. money subtracted from your salary
   c. combined net and gross pay

How Do You Find Your Net Pay After Deductions?

Suppose you're working in a kennel, feeding and bathing animals. You also walk some of the animals. You like your job a lot. You always wanted to have a lot of pets. And now you have 10 pets all at once.

You earn $6.50 an hour, and you work 40 hours per week. This means you earn $1,040 every four weeks. Here is how your earnings statement may look:

Name: Stu Green		Social Security Number: 999-99-9999	
Gross Pay	Federal Tax	FICA	Net Pay
$1,040.00	$114.00	$78.10	$847.90

You started out with gross pay of $1,040. You ended up with net pay of $847.90. What happened? To figure out your net pay, subtract your deductions from your gross pay. First you'll need to add your deductions together to find the total amount.

Solve It

Here's a Tip: To figure your salary for four weeks, you need to answer these questions. What is my hourly wage? How many hours do I work a week? How much do I earn in a week? How much in four weeks?

$$
\begin{array}{ll}
\$\ 114.00 & \text{Federal Income Tax} \\
+\ 78.10 & \text{FICA} \\
\hline
\$\ \text{---} & \text{Total Amount of Deductions}
\end{array}
$$

Then you subtract your deductions from your gross pay. This gives you your net pay.

$$
\begin{array}{ll}
\$1,040.00 & \text{Gross Pay} \\
- & \text{Deductions} \\
\hline
\$\ \text{---} & \text{Net Pay}
\end{array}
$$

Suppose you work for the New American Computer Company. You get paid once a month. The company takes all these deductions from your check: federal tax, state tax, Social Security (FICA), health insurance, and United Fund.

This is the way your earnings statement may look:

Name: Leroy Johnson				Social Security Number: 999-65-4321		
Monthly Gross Pay	Federal Tax	State Tax	FICA	Health Insurance	United Fund	Net Pay
$1,274.00	$150.00	$21.25	$92.71	$114.00	$2.00	$

There is one amount missing. It is your net pay. To find the amount of your net pay, you'll need to add up the deductions and find their total. Then you'll subtract that total from your gross pay.

Progress Check 2

Write your answers on a separate piece of paper.

1. Find out your net pay for one month on the job at the New American Computer Company.

2. What will be the amount of your yearly net pay? (12 x your net pay for one month)

3. If you lived in another state, you might not need to pay state tax. What would be your deductions without state tax?

4. What are you giving to the United Fund in a year?

On the next page are the **earnings statements** for four employees. Each earnings statement is for one month of work.

You'll notice that each person is working in a different place. Each person also has different deductions withheld from gross pay.

Beanstalk Nursery Company
Pay Period Ending: 11/30

Employee: Al Canelli
Social Security Number: 999-00-9999

Gross Pay	Federal Tax	State Tax	FICA	Health Insurance	Disability Insurance	Union Dues	Credit Union	United Fund	Net Pay
$970.00	$108.00	$10.05	$72.85	$114.00					—

Trish's T-Shirt Factory
Pay Period Ending: 3/31

Employee: Lisa Orlando
Social Security Number: 999-01-0009

Gross Pay	Federal Tax	State Tax	FICA	Health Insurance	Disability Insurance	Union Dues	Credit Union	United Fund	Net Pay
$1,126.00	$132.00		$84.56	$114.00	$13.51		$10.50	$3.00	—

Go and Glow Electrical Contractors
Pay Period Ending: 6/30

Employee: Jack Lytell
Social Security Number: 999-12-3456

Gross Pay	Federal Tax	State Tax	FICA	Health Insurance	Disability Insurance	Union Dues	Credit Union	United Fund	Net Pay
$1,280.00	$150.00	$21.25	$96.13			$36.50			—

Jetset Travel Agency
Pay Period Ending: 8/31

Employee: Sarah Greenspan
Social Security Number: 999-88-7777

Gross Pay	Federal Tax	State Tax	FICA	Health Insurance	Disability Insurance	Union Dues	Credit Union	United Fund	Net Pay
$1,266.00	$150.00		$95.08						—

Progress Check 3

Basics Practice

a. $16.41
        39.99
  + 147.02

b. $895.07
  − 300.13

c. $667.05
      x 12

d.   25 ⟌ 625

Read each earnings statement. Notice the gross pay and the deductions on each statement. Then write your answers on a separate piece of paper.

1. Which of the employees do not live in a state that withholds state tax?

2. Who paid union dues?

3. Who had money deducted to repay a loan from the credit union?

4. For each employee, add the deductions. Then subtract the deductions from gross pay. What is the net pay for each employee? List the net pay next to each name.

5. Whose net pay was the highest? Was that person's gross pay the highest? Why did that person have the highest net pay?

6. What will Al Canelli's net pay be for one year?

7. Can the net pay of any employee ever be higher than the gross pay? Why or why not?

8. If Lisa Orlando is sick and cannot work, will she get paid something anyway? Why or why not?

How Do You Figure Percentages of Your Gross Pay?

Suppose you're working as a cook at Tico's Coffee Shop. Your gross pay is $1,033.00 a month. You pay federal income tax, FICA, and health insurance. Here are the amounts you pay:

federal income tax	$113.63
FICA	$82.64
health insurance	$123.96

Here's a chart that shows how your gross pay has been divided.

Here's a Tip: The percentages on this type of chart will always add up to 100%.

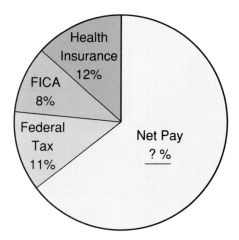

Progress Check 4

Write your answers on a separate piece of paper. Base your answers on the chart above.

1. Look at the deductions. Add up the percentages of the deductions. What is the total percentage of deductions?
2. Subtract the percentage of the deductions from 100%. This will give you the percentage of your pay that you take home. What is that percentage?

More Practice with Percentages

Stanley's gross pay is $1,000. His deductions are $300. What percentage of his gross pay are his deductions? Find out by dividing $300 by $1,000.

$$300 \div 1,000 = 0.30 = 30\%$$

What happens when you divide a small amount by a larger amount? The answer will be a part of a whole, or a fraction of 100. You'll have to use a decimal to show this. Then you must turn the decimal number into a percentage, like this:

.25 = 25%   .37 = 37%   .08 = 8%

Sometimes you'll need to round your answers. Ask: Should the second number after the decimal stay the same or be one number higher? It will depend on the number that follows.

If the third number to the right of the decimal is 4 or lower, cross it off. The number beside it stays the same:

.34$\underline{2}$ = .3$\underline{4}$ = 34%

If the number is 5 or higher, add 1 to the number beside it.

.34$\underline{5}$ = .35 = 35%

If there are other numbers on the right, cross them off. Focus only on the third number to the right of the decimal.

.33$\underline{3}$33 = .33 = 33%

.24$\underline{7}$9 = .25 = 25%

.24$\underline{4}$9 = .24 = 24%

Calculator Practice

What percentage is 500 of 1,500? Here's how to find the answer on your calculator:

Enter 500

Then press the ÷ key.

Enter 1500

Press =

Your answer should be: .33333333 or 33%.

Now find what percentage is 250 of 1,500.

Enter 250.

Then press the ÷ key.

Enter 1500.

Press the = key. What do you get?

Round off this number. The answer is ? %.

Progress Check 5

Write your answers on a separate piece of paper.

1. Kim's gross monthly pay for working as a custodian at the school district is $1,547. Her deductions are $489. What percentage of her gross pay are her deductions? (489 ÷ 1547 = % of gross pay)

2. Uri's gross pay at the movie theater is $525 a month. His deductions are $192. What percentage of his gross pay are his deductions? (192 ÷ 525 = % of gross pay)

3. Cory has a part-time job as a lifeguard. She earns $225 a month. Her deductions are $91. What is her net pay? ($225.00 − $91.00 = net pay) What percentage of her gross pay is her net pay? (net pay ÷ gross pay)

4. Wallace cooks at Tico's Coffee Shop. His gross pay is $1,033 a month. He pays $113.63 in federal tax, $82.64 for Social Security, and $123.96 for health insurance each month. What are his total deductions?

5. Melinda works at another Tico's Coffee Shop in a different state. She earns $1,033 a month in gross pay. These amounts are withheld from her paycheck: $113.63 for federal tax, $82.64 for Social Security, $29.66 for state tax, and $123.96 for health insurance. What percentage of her gross pay are her deductions?

Solve It

Bernie the Bellhop gets his first job at the Insideout Inn. Follow Bernie's income from start to finish for one week. You can do this by reading the boxes from 1 to 12. Write the missing answers on a separate piece of paper.

1. Bernie finds out the bellhop job is open at the Insideout Inn. It pays $4.75 an hour.	**2.** Bernie asks how many hours a week the new bellhop will work. The answer is 30 hours.	**3.** Bernie takes the job.	**4.** Bernie's gross pay for a week is $_____.
5. Bernie's deductions are 30% of his weekly gross pay. The amount of his deductions is $_____.	**6.** Bernie's net pay for the week is $99.75. (Bernie's not very happy about this.)	**7.** But Bernie remembers he earned $60.00 a day in tips. In one 5-day week, he earned $ _____ in tips.	**8.** Bernie adds his tips to his net pay and he gets $_____. (Bernie's feeling better about his job now.)
9. Bernie spends 10% of his net pay on a date the same night he gets paid. The date costs $_____.	**10.** What does Bernie have left for the rest of the week? $_____	**11.** In the next 6 days, Bernie spends $292.68 on fixed and variable expenses.	**12.** How much does Bernie have left when the second week begins? $_____

Can You Figure Out This Income?

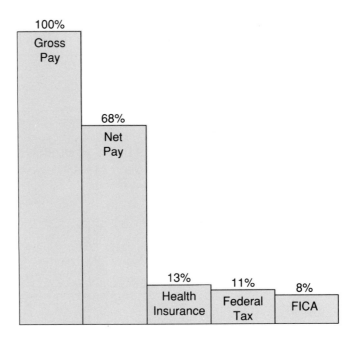

Look at this bar graph. It shows the percentages of each part of an income. Read each one.

Basics Practice

a. 15.25
    x 40 hours

b. 20% of 465 =

c. 10% of 200 =

d. $363.99
    −111.33

Progress Check 6

Write your answers on a separate piece of paper.

1. What percentage of the gross pay is the net pay?
2. Which deduction is the smallest percentage of the gross pay?
3. Add the percentages of all the deductions (13% + 11% + 8%). What is the total?
4. Add the percentage of the net pay to the total percentage of the deductions. Does that equal 100% of the gross pay?

Math on the Job

1. Al Canelli is the shopping clerk at the Beanstalk Nursery. Al has to mark down how many boxes of bean plants are shipped. Today 8 trucks each took 250 boxes. The 9th truck only took 183 boxes. How many boxes will Al mark down on his shipping list?

2. Lisa Orlando orders packing bags for the T-shirts made at her factory. Each T-shirt goes into a bag. Lisa has to order bags every six months. The factory makes 2,500 T-shirts a month. How many bags will Lisa order?

3. Sarah Greenspan is selling airplane tickets for Jetset Travel Agency. There is a special discount of 25%. Sarah has to figure how much to deduct from each ticket for the discount. How much does she need to deduct from a ticket to Canada for $480.40?

4. Jack Lytell is a billing clerk at Go and Glow Electrical Contractors. Jack bills customers for costs of materials and labor on each job. For one job, he is adding $250.00 for labor, $92.52 for wire, $22.50 for switches and plugs, and $20.66 for safety boxes. When Jack finishes adding these costs, how much will the bill be?

5. Paul Chang is foreman of a paving crew. The crew is paving a 10-mile stretch of road. Paul has 4 days to get the job done. He knows the crew can pave 2.5 miles a day. Will the crew get the job done in time?

Chapter Review

Chapter Summary

- Gross pay is the amount of money you earn before deductions.

- A deduction can be subtracted from your salary in any amount.

- Deductions pay for taxes, benefits, services, and memberships.

- The two most common deductions are federal income tax and FICA, or Social Security.

- Salaries and deductions are not the same for all employees. For example, the amount deducted for federal taxes depends on how many allowances you claim.

- You can claim one allowance if you support yourself. You can claim two allowances if you support yourself and someone else.

- To find your net pay, subtract your deductions from your gross pay.

- To find the percentage of gross pay that goes toward deductions, you divide the total deductions by the gross pay.

Chapter Quiz

Write your answers on a separate sheet of paper.

1. These deductions are taken from Saul's salary: federal income tax $114.00, FICA $78.00, union dues $22.00, state income tax $12.00. What is the total amount of Saul's deductions?

2. Which of these deductions are paid by almost everybody who works?

    a. federal income tax   b. credit union

    c. United Fund   d. FICA

3. Julie's gross pay is $1,008.71. Her deductions total $386.00. What is her net pay?

4. Gloria's net pay is $780.92 a month. Her deductions total $256.26. What is her gross pay?

5. If Roger's deductions are 44% of his gross pay, what percentage will his net pay be?

6. Which of these is not found on an earnings statement?

    a. name

    b. telephone number

    c. gross pay

7. Clyde is doing exactly the same work at the factory as his friend Keith. Both work the same amount of time. Both have been there one year. Their gross pay is the same, but Clyde's net pay is higher than Keith's. What could make a difference in their salaries?

8. Annie's gross pay is $1,111.00. Her deductions are $411.00. What percentage of Annie's gross pay are her deductions? How much would 50% be?

Challenge

Use the earnings statements on page 58 to make one of your own. It can be for a real or invented job. Be sure to show all deductions and the correct net pay. Remember to put in your name and Social Security number.

Unit Two Review

Answer the following questions on a separate piece of paper. Look back at Chapters 3 and 4 if you need help.

1. What are three ways of looking for a job?

2. What is a wage? Are all wages the same?

3. How do you figure your income?

4. What is your net pay? How do you figure it?

5. What are deductions? Why are they taken out of your paycheck?

6. Do you use gross income or net income when you figure your budget? Why?

7. What is overtime pay?

8. What is one way employees keep track of their working hours?

9. What is the difference between a weekly wage and a monthly wage?

10. What is an earnings statement?

Unit Three

Banking and Saving

5 Choosing a Bank

Bank tellers can usually answer any questions you have about your account.

Chapter Learning Objectives

- Identify and list your banking needs.
- Compare three types of checking accounts.
- Identify the checking account that fits a particular income and budget.
- Compare three types of savings accounts.
- Review basic math skills in the Appendix at the back of this textbook.

Words to Know

ATM   Automated Teller Machine, a walk-up computer station on the outside of the bank; machine used by a bank customer to make deposits and withdrawals

balance   the money left in a bank account

bank account   bank record of the money a customer deposits and withdraws

deposit   to put money into a bank account; money put into a bank account

interest   the amount it costs to use money that is lent

monthly service charge   a bank's fee for taking care of an account

teller   a person who works in a bank helping customers with deposits, withdrawals, and check-cashing

withdrawal   money taken out of a bank account

Why Put Your Money in a Bank?

You have an income. You have a budget. You're paying your bills. But do you go to the electric company to pay in person? Or to the phone company? Do you pay your bills with cash or expensive money orders?

If you do, you might want to think about putting your paycheck in a bank. Then you can write checks to pay your bills and send your checks by mail. This will save you a lot of time and energy.

They're Not All the Same: Your money helps banks make money. Some offer certain services to get your business. Others charge for the same services. It pays to shop for your bank just as you would for a car.

Also, a bank will pay you money if you keep your savings there. And loans are easier to get if you have a **bank account**. Banks lend money for cars and other things.

There are three main kinds of banks: commercial banks, savings banks, and credit unions. Any of the three kinds may be a full-service bank. A full-service bank offers checking and savings accounts, **ATM (Automated Teller Machine)**, and loans.

What Do You Need from a Bank?

It helps to choose a bank you can get to easily. You'll also want a bank that offers good bargains on its accounts.

Banks have different kinds of accounts to fit different kinds of income. Choosing the best account for you is important. Find out what you need from a bank. First, find out about your checking needs.

Progress Check 1

Write your answers on a separate piece of paper.

1. Imagine you're working at a factory and sharing an apartment with a friend. How many regular monthly payments will you make? (Examples: rent, electricity, telephone.) Write down as many as you can think of. Then count them.
2. How many regular weekly expenses could you pay by check? (Example: groceries.) Count these expenses. Now multiply your total by 4, because there are about four weeks in a month.

3. Will you have any monthly loan payments?
   (Examples: car, TV set.) Write these down and
   count them.

4. Add the amounts for questions 1, 2, and 3 above.
   This gives you the number of checks you will write
   in a month. What is the total?

It's important to know how many checks you need to
write each month. This helps you decide what kind of
checking account will be best for you. Read the chart
below. It describes three kinds of checking accounts.
Look for the differences. Also notice that keeping a
high **balance** sometimes earns extra money for you.
This extra money is called **interest**.

Type of Account	Charge for each check you write	Monthly Service Charge	Interest paid for keeping a $1000 balance
Budget Checking	First 4 free, then 75¢ per check	$2.50	None
Regular Checking	12¢ per check	$6.00	None
Interest-Paying Checking	All checks free	$7.50	$4.00 per month

Progress Check 2

1. If you write 11 checks a month, what will it cost
   to use Budget Checking? (Multiply the charge for
   each check by the number of checks you'll write.
   Don't forget that the first four checks are free!)
   Copy that cost on your paper. Then add the
   monthly service charge. The total shows how
   much it will cost each month to use Budget
   Checking.

Wordwise: The *monthly service charge* is the money you pay the bank each month for taking care of your account.

2. Which costs less—writing 11 checks from Budget Checking or 11 checks from Regular Checking? How much less?

3. Suppose that each month you **deposit** $50 more than you spend. How many months will it take to build up a $1,000 balance? (You'll need to divide $1,000 by $50.)

4. A $1,000 balance pays you $4.00 per month in interest. Does that make Interest-Paying Checking cheaper than Regular Checking?

5. Until you reach a $1,000 balance, which is the best account for you?

How Do You Find the Best Bank for You?

You've decided you want a Regular Checking account. But different banks have different charges for their Regular Checking accounts. How will you choose?

Call on two or three banks in your neighborhood. Find out what the monthly charges are for regular checking accounts. Then choose the one that suits you best.

The chart below describes three Regular Checking accounts.

Comparing Regular Checking Accounts

	Charge for each check you write	Monthly Service Charge	Balance needed to avoid service charge
Bank A	First 2 free, then 44¢ per check	$4.00	$500.00
Bank B	12¢ per check	$6.00	$500.00
Bank C	None	$8.75	No requirement

Progress Check 3

Here's a Tip: Follow these steps to find how much you'll pay for Regular Checking.
1. Find the cost for 11 checks a month. (Remember, Bank A gives 2 free.)
2. Then add the monthly service charge.

Write your answers on a separate piece of paper.

1. You will write 11 checks per month. What will Bank A's account cost you?
2. What will Bank B's account cost you each month?
3. What will Bank C's account cost you each month?
4. Compare Banks A, B, and C. Which account is the best one for you?
5. If you had a $500 balance, which account would be the best one for you?

Could You Use a Safe-Deposit Box?

Suppose your aunt gave you a savings bond now worth $125. Or your grandmother gave you a special piece of family jewelry. These things might get lost or stolen in your apartment. And what about your birth certificate? The receipt for your car? A passport? Special pictures and papers? In a fire, those could be destroyed.

You can rent a safe-deposit box at your bank. A safe-deposit box is a very secure place to store valuable things. Safe-deposit boxes are locked in fireproof rooms behind heavy steel doors.

Banks have different sizes of safe-deposit boxes. The regular size costs about $15 a year.

Progress Check 4

Write your answers on a separate piece of paper.

1. Rent for a safe-deposit box is $15 a year. How much does that cost per month?

2. A metal lockbox for your home cost $1.50 a month for 12 months. What is the total price of the lockbox? Does the lockbox cost more than the safe-deposit box? What's the difference in cost?

3. You have decided to get a large safe-deposit box. The rent is $30 a year. The bank will let you divide your rent into 12 monthly payments. How much will each payment be?

What Is an ATM? How Does It Work?

Customers often stand in line in a bank. They have to wait to do business with the **tellers** behind the counter. Tellers help customers with deposits, **withdrawals**, and check-cashing. If you have questions to ask a teller, it is usually worth waiting in line.

Most banks also have Automated Teller Machines, called ATMs. ATMs work 24 hours a day, even when the bank is closed. There's usually no waiting in line, but you can't expect an ATM to answer your questions.

You'll especially like the ATM if the bank is open only while you're at work. With ATMs you can make deposits or get cash at night and on weekends.

You can get an ATM operating card when you open your checking account. It's a plastic card with a secret code that you memorize.

The ATM has a slot where you insert the card. You must push the right buttons for your code. Then the machine waits for you to tell it what to do. You press buttons to give directions to the machine.

Some banks charge you for using the ATM. The charge might be about 20¢ for every ATM withdrawal. Make sure you ask about this when you choose your bank.

Basics Practice

a. $12\overline{)\$36.00}$

b. $$\begin{array}{r} \$2.50 \\ \times\ \ 12 \\ \hline \end{array}$$

c. $12\overline{)\$10.80}$

d. $$\begin{array}{r} \$4.25 \\ \times\ \ 12 \\ \hline \end{array}$$

If you are charged for using your ATM card, you'll need to keep track of the charges. Otherwise, you may think you have more money in your account than you really have.

Calculator Practice

Perry used the ATM 24 times in one month for withdrawals. How much did this cost him, if his bank charged 20¢ each time?

Enter 24

Press x

Enter .20

Press =

Your answer should be: $4.80

Money Orders

Suppose you don't have a checking account. If you plan to pay any bills by mail, never send cash. Instead, buy money orders. They are just as safe to send in the mail as a check.

You can buy money orders at banks. Sometimes money orders are called by different names, such as *cashier's checks*.

You can also buy money orders at the post office or at stores that cash paychecks.

No matter where you buy them, money orders are expensive. Each one costs at least $2. Sometimes the bigger the money order, the more it costs.

What if you pay several bills by mail each month? Using money orders can cost you a lot. It might pay to get a checking account, instead.

Progress Check 5

Write your answers on a separate piece of paper.

Here's a Tip: Banks sell Travelers' Checks, sometimes spelled *cheques*. These come in amounts of $10, $20, $50, or $100 each. If they're lost or stolen, they're replaced for free.

1. You use money orders to pay five bills a month by mail. Money orders cost $2 each. How much do your five money orders cost? Copy the answer. Label it *Money Orders*. Go on to question 2.

2. Budget Checking accounts are for people who don't write many checks every month. Suppose a budget account has a monthly service charge of $2.50. The account offers four free checks per month. If you write more than four, they cost 75¢ each. Because you are writing five checks, add 75¢ to the service charge. Write the total on your paper and label it *Budget Checking*.

3. Suppose a Regular Checking account has a $6 monthly service charge. Each check you write in this account costs 38¢. How much will it cost to write five checks a month? (Multiply the cost of the checks by 5, and add the service charge.) Write the total on your paper, and label it *Regular Checking*.

4. Is a checking account cheaper than money orders? How much less does Budget Checking cost? How much less is the Regular Checking account?

Want to See Your Money Grow? Try Savings.

For big purchases, such as cars, you'll need to save or borrow money. If you borrow, you'll pay interest while paying back the loan.

Paying interest to a bank is like paying rent to use loan money. The interest you pay is a percentage of your loan. Sometimes it is as high as 21%. That is more than one-fifth of the loan!

If you save, you'll receive interest. The bank will pay interest to you on a savings account. The interest you receive is a percentage of your savings.

Suppose you have extra money each month. Even if it's not much, you can put it into a savings account. It will grow in the bank because the interest will be added to it. The money will be there for you when you have something special to buy.

Many people have both a checking account and a savings account. In fact, you can have them both in one account. An interest-paying checking account is both a checking and a savings account. It is a savings account that lets you write checks.

To have a combined checking-savings account, you must keep a large, steady bank balance. For example, you might need to keep $1000 in the account that you never spend. If your balance drops below $1000, the bank can stop paying you interest and might take out money for service charges.

Calculator Practice

Figuring percentages can be done with a calculator. The symbol % means percent. Percents are parts of 100. One hundred percent (100%) means *total*. Fifty percent is *half*, 33% is *one-third*, 25% is *one-fourth*, or a *quarter*.

Suppose you don't want to pay more than 25% of your income for rent. Your monthly paycheck is $604.80. *(continued on next page)*

Enter 604.80 on the calculator.

Press x for multiplication.

Enter 25.

Press the % key.

Press the = key.

The answer is $151.20, which is 25% of your paycheck.

How much is 50% of 6? Use your calculator to find out.

Use Percentages to Figure Out Interest

Interest is the money the bank pays you for keeping your savings there. Interest is a percentage of your savings. It is figured for one year. There are 12 months in a year. To figure out one month's interest, you divide the yearly total by 12.

You can figure percents by multiplication. First put the percent you want to the right of a decimal point. If the percent you want is less than 10, put a zero in front of it like this: .05. Then multiply by the number you want to find the percentage of.

Suppose you put $480 in a savings account at 5% interest. To figure what you'll earn find 5% of $480. (.05 x 480 = ?) Remember to put the decimal point in the right place! $24 is the annual interest.

Basics Practice

a. $6.05
    x .09

b. $12.00
    x .08

c. 3)$39.00

d. $1.87
    x 4.5

Progress Check 6

Write your answers on a separate piece of paper.

1. What is 6% yearly interest of $400? (Figure .06 x 400 = ?) What is the monthly interest? (Divide the answer by 12.)

2. What is 12% yearly interest of $500? What is 50% (one-half) of the yearly interest? (Multiply the answer by .50.)

3. What is 8% yearly interest of $1,000? What is 25% (one-quarter) of the yearly interest?

Interested in Interest? Here's How to Get It.

All full-service banks offer savings accounts.

The basic savings account is called a *passbook account*. You can save or withdraw your money whenever you wish. The bank teller marks new totals in your passbook each time. Or the ATM will give you a receipt that shows your new savings balance. That lets you know how much you've saved. Passbook accounts pay about 5% interest per year.

Interest-paying checking accounts give slightly lower interest than passbook accounts. Unless there's over $1,000 in the account, you'll pay a monthly service charge. But there is no charge for each check you write.

Here's a Tip: Banks usually pay *compound interest*. Every day they add to your savings. At 5% interest compounded daily, $100 in the bank earns $5.12 every year.

Time Savings accounts give the best deal. But you can't withdraw from Time Savings accounts whenever you want to. Time Savings accounts are often called CD accounts. CD means Certificate of Deposit.

Suppose you have $500 that can sit in the bank for a while. In a CD account for a month, it can earn 7% annual interest. Leave it for three months, the annual interest rate is 8%. At six months, the annual interest rate is 9%.

Remember that these rates are for a year. If you leave the money in for half a year, you'll get half of the annual interest. If you leave it in for a quarter of a year, you'll get one-quarter of the annual interest. Now you can choose which savings account is best for you.

Solve It

What is 7% of $500?

$500
x .07
_____

What is 8% of $500?

$500
x .08
_____

What is 9% of $500?

$500
x .09
_____

Progress Check 7

Answer these questions on a separate piece of paper.

1. You have saved $121.20 in a passbook account. The interest rate is 5%. How much will you earn in a year? (Multiply .05 x 121.20.) How much in one month? (Divide the yearly total by 12 to get the monthly total.) Round off the monthly total.

2. You put $480.28 in a passbook account at 5% interest. How much will you earn in a year? In a month?

3. You put $500.88 in a CD account for three months at 8% yearly interest. How much will you earn during the three months? (Three months is one-fourth of a year. So divide the yearly total by 4 to find the amount.)

4. If you leave your $500.88 deposit for six months, interest is 9%. How much will you earn? (This time divide your yearly total by two. Six months is half a year. Dividing by two gives you one-half. Round off and copy the total.)

Math on the Job

1. Virginia has her company put 3% of her paycheck into savings. If Virginia's salary is $1,232 a month, how much does she save each month?

2. Inez has just sold 14 money orders at $2 each. How much should she collect from the customers for the fees?

3. Jerry works in a bank. He is figuring out the charges on Mr. Endicott's account. Mr. Endicott has written 24 checks. Each check costs 15¢, and there is a $5 service charge. What should Barry deduct from the account?

4. Wanda is a bank teller. Mrs. Frey has just deposited $248 into her savings account that already had $728 in it. Mrs. Frey's account has earned $12.32 in interest since her last deposit. What total should Wanda enter in Mrs. Frey's savings book?

5. Larry and Luann are opening envelopes deposited in the ATM at the bank where they work. The first five envelopes have checks for these amounts: $132.48, $178.92, $48.16, $92.84, and $345.90. What is the total so far?

6. Barbara has $1,200 in her savings account. The bank pays 7% interest. If she makes no deposits or withdrawals during the year, how much money will be in the account at the end of the year?

Chapter Review

Chapter Summary

- Using a bank can make life easier. You can stop running around to pay bills with cash. You can mail checks, instead. Banks have several kinds of checking accounts.

- Most banks have Automated Teller Machines (ATMs). ATMs save waiting in line at the bank. You can deposit or withdraw money at an ATM at night or on weekends, even though the bank is closed.

- Banks will pay you money—called interest—if you deposit money in a savings account. There are several kinds of savings accounts.

- Banks make loans for cars and other costly items.

- Different kinds of bank accounts fit different kinds of income. You need to decide which account is best for you.

- Some checking accounts have a monthly service charge plus a charge for each check. Some charge only for each check. Some checking accounts pay you interest if you deposit enough money and keep a big balance.

- You can buy and mail money orders to pay your bills. Using money orders costs more money than writing checks.

- If you save, the bank pays you interest. If you borrow, you pay the bank interest on top of your loan payments. Saving isn't easy, but it's cheaper than borrowing.

- Time Savings accounts earn more interest than some other kinds of accounts. If you leave your money in the account for at least a month, you get higher interest.

Chapter Quiz

Sandy's bank offers the following services:

Budget Checking: $2.50 monthly service charge, 4 free checks, and additional checks cost 75¢ each.

Regular Checking: $5.00 monthly service charge, 22¢ per check. The service charge is dropped if you keep a $500 balance.

Passbook Savings: $1.50 monthly service charge, 5% interest. The service charge is dropped if you keep a $200 balance.

Time Savings: For a deposit of $500, this account pays 7% yearly interest for a month, 8% for three months, 9% for six months.

Write your answers on a separate sheet of paper.

1. If Sandy writes five checks per month, what will Budget Checking cost?

2. If Sandy writes five checks per month, what will Regular Checking cost?

3. If Sandy writes 11 checks per month, which costs more— Budget or Regular?

4. Money orders cost $2 each. If Sandy buys 5 money orders a month, would using Regular Checking be cheaper than writing money orders? How much?

5. Suppose Sandy puts $400 in a Passbook Savings account. How much yearly interest would it earn?

6. Is monthly Passbook interest on $400 higher than the monthly service charge?

7. How much interest would $500 earn in Passbook Savings for 6 months?

8. Sandy earns $800 a month. Sandy wants to save 15% of that. How much will Sandy save in a month?

6 Using a Checking Account

Paying by check is a good way to keep track of where your money goes.

Chapter Learning Objectives

- List the procedures for opening a checking account.
- Fill out a deposit slip.
- Write a check.
- Make entries in a check register.
- Balance a checking account.
- Review basic math skills in the Appendix at the back of this textbook.

Words to Know

authorized   approved; official; correct

bank statement   a bank form that is sent each month to the customer; a form listing all the checks paid, deposits made, ATM uses, service charges, and the account's balance

cancelled check   any check the bank pays and subtracts from your checking account

check register   a small booklet to use to keep track of your balance when you write checks or make a deposit or a withdrawal

currency   folding money; money in bills, such as a dollar bill or a five-dollar bill

deposit slip   a slip of paper kept by the bank to show how much money you put into your account

endorse   to sign your name on the back of a check

entry   something entered into a book or booklet

signature card   a card with the name, address, and authorized signature of a bank customer

How Do You Open a Checking Account?

Suppose you've found a good bank. You've thought about different checking accounts. You've decided on the checking account that best fits your budget. You're ready to open your account. What is the first step?

There are three things you'll need to do when opening a checking account.

You must:

1. Give the bank certain information.
2. Fill out a **signature card**.
3. Make a deposit to open your account.

What the Bank Needs to Know

Wordwise: If the checking account is for one person, it's called a *single account*. If it's for two people, it's called a *joint account*.

The bank will need to know a few facts about you. You must explain if your account is just for you or for you and another person. You must give your correct name and address. If you have a job, you must also give the name and address of the place where you work. By law, the bank needs your Social Security (or tax identification) number. You will also have to say how much you plan to deposit to open your account.

You will then be asked to sign a signature card. This shows the bank the **authorized**, or official, way you plan to sign your checks. The authorized signature is the only one the bank will accept on your checks.

The Deposit Slip

To put money into your new account, you must fill out a **deposit slip**. The slip should show how much cash you are depositing. It should also show the amount of any checks you deposit. You must then write the total amount of the deposit.

Progress Check 1

Write your answers on a separate piece of paper.

1. Why would the bank need to know your address?
2. Why would the bank need your authorized signature?

How Do You Fill Out a Deposit Slip?

Imagine that this is your deposit slip. You've just filled it out to make your first deposit. You're including **currency**, or folding money, of $60. You're including a check for $35.

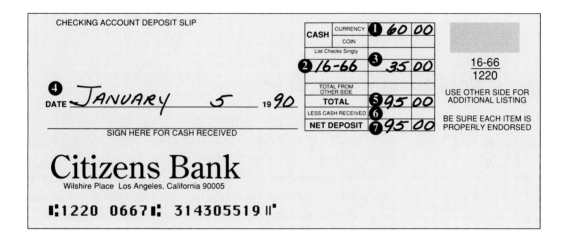

Progress Check 2

The circled numbers on the deposit slip match the sentences below. Answer each question on a separate piece of paper.

1. This shows the amount of currency you deposited. How much currency did you deposit?
2. This is the bank number of the check you put into your account. What is the bank number?
3. This is the amount of the check you deposited. What is that amount?
4. This is the date you made the deposit. What is that date?

Here's a Tip:
The bank number of every check will look something like this:

$$\frac{11\text{-}30}{1222}$$

The number is usually in the upper right portion of the check. You will write the top numbers on your deposit slip.

5. This is the total of the amount you deposited. What is the total?

6. Suppose you deposit a paycheck but need some cash in return. In which space would you write the amount of cash you want back?

7. Which space do you use to show the total deposit less cash received? Would you need to sign the deposit slip if you're getting cash back?

A Word About Writing Checks

When you open an account, the bank will give you some blank checks to use. The bank will add your account number to the checks. But the checks won't be printed with your name and address. Before long, you'll receive your printed checks in the mail. Look the checks over. Ask yourself these questions:

Did You Know?
The check number in the upper right corner is the number you and the bank will use to keep track of the check. The number may be a three- or four-digit number.

- Is my name spelled correctly?
- Are my address and phone number correct?
- Does the account number on the check match the account number on my copy of the signature card? (The account number is in the lower left corner of your check.)
- Is the name and address of the bank correct?
- Are the check numbers in order? For example, do they read 101, 102, 103, and so on?

On the facing page is a filled-out check. It shows the correct way to write a check.

Look at the check carefully. Notice where the date is and to whom the check is written. Look at the amount. It's written in numerals and in words. The check paid for a shirt. The signature is on the check.

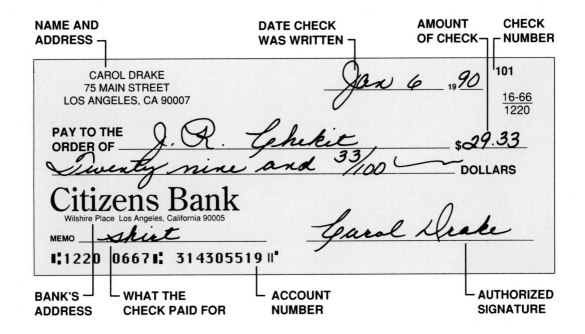

NAME AND ADDRESS

DATE CHECK WAS WRITTEN

AMOUNT OF CHECK

CHECK NUMBER

CAROL DRAKE
75 MAIN STREET
LOS ANGELES, CA 90007

Jan 6 19 90 101

16-66
1220

PAY TO THE ORDER OF ___ J. R. Ghikit ___ $29.33

Twenty nine and 33/100 ___ DOLLARS

Citizens Bank
Wilshire Place Los Angeles, California 90005

MEMO ___ shirt ___

Carol Drake

⑈1220 0667⑈ 314305519 ⑈

BANK'S ADDRESS

WHAT THE CHECK PAID FOR

ACCOUNT NUMBER

AUTHORIZED SIGNATURE

Progress Check 3

Follow each direction below. Write your response on a separate piece of paper.

1. Write today's date the way you would need to write it on a check.

2. Imagine you're writing a check to the classmate seated closest to you in the room. Write that person's name as if you were making out a check to him or her.

3. Your check is for $37.10. Write the amount in numerals and in words. Look at Carol Drake's check above to see how to do this.

4. Sign your name as you would sign a check. Be sure you use your authorized signature.

5. Imagine that you could write a check for any amount to anyone you like. To whom would you write the check and why? What might you write on the check's memo line?

How to Keep Track of the Checks You Write

Along with your checks, you'll get a **check register**. One kind of register looks like the one below. Read each column heading. Then read each **entry** carefully.

CHECK NO	DATE	CHECKS ISSUED TO OR DESCRIPTION OF DEPOSIT	(−) AMOUNT OF CHECK	√ T	(+) AMOUNT OF DEPOSIT	BALANCE
						7 20 00
1 101	**2** 1/6	**3** J.R. CHECKIT	**5** 29 33			**8** 17 67
		4 FOR NEW SHIRT				
—	1/7	DEPOSIT (YARD SALE CASH)	—	—	**6** 90 00	**9** 26 67

Basics Practice

a. $23.14   Food
    275.00   Rent
     12.37   Phone
  + 59.50   Loan

b. $300.15
        x   12

c.   12)144

d. $2,943.78
    − 1,822.39

Progress Check 4

The circled numbers on the check register match the sentences below. Answer the questions on a separate piece of paper.

1. This is the number of the check used. What is the number?

2. This is the date the check was written. What is that date?

3. This is the person or company receiving the check. To whom was the check written?

4. This is the reason the check was written. What did the check pay for?

5. This is the amount of the check. What is the amount?

6. This is the amount of a deposit. What is that amount? On what date was the deposit made?
7. This was the beginning balance. It was the amount in the account before writing the check or making the deposit. What is this amount?
8. This was the balance after subtracting the check for $29.33. What is that balance?
9. This shows the balance after the deposit of $90. What is the new balance?

Balancing Your Checking Account

Did You Know?
Sign your authorized signature when you endorse a check for deposit. Add *For Deposit Only.* To be safe, add your account number, too. Then no one else will get your deposit by accident.

It's very important to know how much money you have in your checking account. Each time you write a check, record it in your register. Then subtract the amount of the check from your balance. Write the new balance.

If you make a deposit, write it in the register, too. Add the amount of the deposit to find your new balance. Write the new balance in your register.

Here is an example of how your check register might look. Only the balances are missing.

CHECK NO	DATE	CHECKS ISSUED TO OR DESCRIPTION OF DEPOSIT	(−) AMOUNT OF CHECK		√ T	(+) AMOUNT OF DEPOSIT	BALANCE	
							210	00
266	10/1	PETE'S DINER	6	50			—	
		LUNCH						
267	10/2	CENTRAL ELECTRIC	32	00			—	
		ELECTRICITY BILL						
—	10/2	DEPOSIT	—	—		150	00	—

Progress Check 5

You'll need to read the check register on page 93 to answer the questions below. Write your answers on a separate piece of paper.

1. Your beginning balance is $210.00. What is your balance after paying for your lunch at Pete's Diner?
2. What is your balance after paying your electricity bill?
3. What is your balance after depositing $150.00 to your account? (Always add your deposits.)

Basics Practice

a.
$$\begin{array}{r} \$520.00 \\ -2.19 \\ \hline \end{array}$$

b.
$$\begin{array}{r} \$111.20 \\ +312.00 \\ \hline \end{array}$$

c.
$$\begin{array}{r} \$133.04 \\ -8.39 \\ \hline \end{array}$$

d.
$$\begin{array}{r} \$62.86 \\ -9.00 \\ \hline \end{array}$$

Solve It

1. Barry thought he had $150 in his checking account. He didn't. He forgot to record a check he wrote for $45. How much money does Barry really have in his account?
2. If you write a check for more money that you have in your account, the check will bounce. The bank will not honor the check. The bank will, instead, charge your account a fee for withdrawing too much money. Barry's next check is for $125. He has made no deposits. The $125 check will bounce. The bank will subtract a $10 fee for the bounced check. By how much will Barry be short?

Your Bank Statement

At the end of each month, the bank mails a **bank statement** to each of its checking account customers. The statement shows how many checks have been cashed. It shows how many deposits you made. It lists any service charges.

It tells you how much you have in your account.

Read all the items on the Buckeye Bank statement. Read the information in these sections: checks, other charges, deposits. Notice the ending balance.

Buckeye Bank
Fountain Square, Cincinnati, Ohio 45202

C.D. Player
333 HiFi Way
Discville, OH 45221

Closing Date: 9/28/89 ❶

Beginning Balance: 397.67 ❷

Checking Account Number 314159265

CHECKS

Check Number	Date Paid	Amount	Check Number	Date Paid	Amount
221	9/6/89	52.98			
222	9/7/89	20.20			
223	9/10/89	6.92			
224	9/13/89	10.23 ❸			
225	9/13/89	35.00			
226	9/18/89	29.12			
228	9/21/89	45.90			

OTHER CHARGES

	Date Paid	Amount
❹ Service Charge	9/28/89	5.00

DEPOSITS

Date	Amount	Date	Amount
❺ 9/28/89	225.98		

Ending Balance: 418.30 ❻

Progress Check 6

Here's a Tip:
Sometimes a star on the bank statement marks the place of a check that hasn't been cashed or written yet. The check is missing from the numbered order.

The numbers on the Buckeye Bank statement match the numbers of the descriptions below. Read each description. Then answer the questions on a separate piece of paper.

1. This is the date the bank statement was made. What is the date?
2. This is the beginning balance. What is the amount?
3. These are the checks cashed. The check number, the date the bank paid each one, and the amount of each check are listed. How many checks were cashed?
4. This is the service charge. How much is it?
5. This is the amount of the deposit for the month. How much is it?
6. This is the ending balance. It is the amount in the account after the checks, service charge, and deposits have been figured. What is the ending balance?

Calculator Practice

Use your calculator to add up all the checks that were cashed.

Enter 52.98	Press +
Enter 20.20	Press +
Enter 6.92	Press +
Enter 10.23	Press +
Enter 35.00	Press +
Enter 29.12	Press +
Enter 45.90	Press =

Your answer should be: $200.35

How Do You Balance Your Checkbook?

Here are ten steps you can follow to balance your checkbook.

1. Update your checkbook. Find your current balance. Add all deposits you haven't yet added. Subtract any checks you haven't already subtracted. Then subtract all service charges found on your bank statement. Record the updated balance.

Wordwise: A *cancelled* check has already been cashed by the bank. It is mailed back to you with your statement. Checks that have not reached the bank are called *outstanding* checks.

2. Arrange the **cancelled checks** sent along with your bank statement. Place them in numbered order (by date or by check number).

3. Compare the cancelled checks to the ones listed on your statement. Check off each one on the statement.

4. List all the checks you wrote in your check register that haven't been cancelled at the bank. Add them together.

5. Compare the deposits listed on your bank statement with the ones you listed in your check register. Check off each deposit on the statement.

6. List all the deposits from your check register that do not appear on your statement. Add them together.

7. Write down the ending balance from your bank statement.

8. Add to that the total of all deposits not yet recorded by the bank.

9. Subtract from that the total of all checks that have not yet been cashed.

10. Your final answer should match your updated checkbook balance. If it doesn't, you will know that someone (either you or the bank) has made a mistake.

Progress Check 7

Look back at the Buckeye Bank statement to answer these questions. Write your answers on a separate piece of paper.

1. C. D. Player's checkbook register shows that she has a balance of $550. From this she subtracts the bank's service charge. What should her updated balance be? Write the amount and label it *Updated Register Balance.*

2. Ms. Player sees that check #227 has not been cancelled. The check is for $45.30. She subtracts this from the ending balance shown on her bank statement. What will be her new ending balance?

3. To the new ending balance, she adds the $172 deposit she made after the bank statement was printed. Now what is her new ending balance? Does it match her updated register balance? (See your answer for item 1.)

What If Your Checking Account Doesn't Balance?

Suppose you try to balance your checking account, but it doesn't balance. There are ways to figure out what the problem is. Here are some questions to help you.

1. Did you mark off every check that was returned?
2. Did you make any mistakes in addition or subtraction?
3. Did you subtract the service charge from your checkbook balance?

Basics Practice

a. $7.22
   18.30
   19.01
 + 44.92

b. $832.00
  − 99.94

c. $1,387.54
   3,965.00
 + 876.28

d. $7,362.75
 − 1,433.87

Solve It

		Balance
Water Company	$33.00	$173.00
Service Charge	$6.00	
Sporting Goods	$13.00	$160.00

Can you find the error? What is it?

4. Did you add all recent deposits to the ending balance on your statement?

5. Did the bank add and subtract correctly? Check the figures on the bank statement.

If the answers to these questions do not show the problem, ask for help from your bank. Take your statement, cancelled checks, and checkbook register along with you. A teller can help find the correct balance.

Math on the Job

1. Linda Wong is a bank teller. A customer deposits a $100.00 check and asks for $43.50 back in cash. How much will Linda deposit in the customer's bank account?

2. Charlie Smith is a gardener. He needs a new $365.00 lawn mower. He has $150.00 in his bank account. Then he deposits checks for $56.00, $46.00, $78.00, $35.00, and $58.00. If he writes a check for the lawn mower, how much will he have left in his account?

Chapter Review

Chapter Summary

- To open a checking account, you will need to do three things: give the bank certain information, fill out a signature card, and make a deposit to your account.

- You must fill out a deposit slip each time you make a deposit to your account. All cash and check amounts must be listed, along with each check's bank number.

- When you receive printed checks in the mail, you need to look them over. All information printed on your checks must be correct.

- It is important to know how much money you have in your checking account. Keep good records in your checkbook register.
  - Write the date and amount of each check you pay out.
  - Subtract each check from your balance.
  - Record each deposit you make.
  - Add each deposit to your balance.

- Each month, your bank will send you your cancelled checks and a statement. Use the statement to correct and update your balance on your check register.

- If your checking account doesn't balance, there are several ways to find your error. You need to go back over all ten steps for figuring your balance. Someone at your bank can help you if you cannot find your errors.

Chapter Quiz

Read each description below. Tell what is missing from each description. Write your answers on a separate sheet of paper.

1. You go to open a checking account. You answer the questions the new accounts person asks you. You fill out and sign a signature card. What else do you need to do?

2. You deposit a check for $168. You want to receive $68 back in cash. You write the bank number and amount on the deposit slip. You endorse the check and hand the deposit slip to the teller. What else do you need to do?

3. You write a check for $33.17. You write the amount in numerals on the check. What other way do you need to write $33.17?

4. You make an entry in your check register. You mark the number and date of the check. You list the person receiving the check as well as the reason. You record the amount of the check. What else should you do?

5. You add up these deposits. What did you forget to do?

$$\begin{array}{r} \$11.13 \\ 66.00 \\ + \ 10.00 \\ \hline \$ \ 7.13 \end{array}$$

Challenge

Get a blank check register from a bank. Write in a made-up balance. Then enter some invented checks, deposits, and ATM withdrawals. Figure each new balance. Recheck your math for errors. Use a calculator, if you have one.

Unit Three Review

Read each set of statements below. Only one of the statements, a or b, is true. On another piece of paper, write the numbers 1 to 6. Then write the letter of the true statement. Rewrite the false statement to make it true.

1. a. Banks pay you for saving money.
   b. The only service banks offer is checking accounts.

2. a. Checking accounts are usually free to the customer.
   b. Using checks is a cheap and easy way to pay bills.

3. a. Writing a check takes money out of your account.
   b. To put money into your account, all you do is give the bank some cash.

4. a. You should record all checks you write and all deposits you make. Then you will know how much money you have in your checking account.
   b. On your bank statement, your checks and bank charges are subtracted from your deposits.

5. a. You must pay your bills in person with cash if you don't have a checking account.
   b. A safe-deposit box is a secure way to store your valuables.

6. a. You must use a deposit slip when you are adding money to your account.
   b. Only make entries in your check register when you receive your bank statement.

Unit Four

Selecting Housing

7 Finding a Place to Live

The classified ads in a newspaper list many apartments and houses for rent.

Chapter Learning Objectives

- Figure the amount of a given salary that should go to pay for rent.
- Interpret a classified ad for an apartment.
- Compare rents and rental terms.
- Figure the amount of a refund from a security deposit and the cost of breaking a lease.
- Compare a variety of rental situations and figure the cost of each one.
- Review basic math skills in the Appendix at the back of this textbook.

Words to Know

abbreviated made shorter

ad a short form of the word *advertisement*

deposit money a renter may have to pay before moving in; money that will be returned when the renter moves out if the place is clean and has not been damaged

lease a written agreement between a renter and the owner of the place being rented

refund money returned from a deposit or other money paid out

rental application an information form filled out by someone who wants to rent property

What About Location?

Finding a place to live can be a real challenge. First you need to decide on the location that would be best for you. Your life will be much easier if you can find a place that isn't too far from:

- your job (or school).
- the bus line (if you don't have your own transportation).
- a grocery store.

You might ask yourself these questions: How many miles away from my job can I live? What will transportation cost to go to and from work or school? Are there stores and shops nearby?

Sylvester works downtown. But he wants to get an apartment in the section of town where his brother lives.

Here's a Tip: Use a map of the city or town where you plan to live. Outline the section where you'll look for a place to live. Decide which streets and neighborhoods you'll include in that section.

That neighborhood is 15 miles from Sylvester's job. How many miles will he travel to and from work in a day? (2 x 15 miles = 30 miles) How many miles will he travel in a month? Most people usually work about 22 days in a month. Multiply 22 by the number of miles Sylvester travels each day.

Solve It

How many miles will Sylvester travel to work in a month of 22 working days?

Number of days he works		Number of miles he travels in a day	
_____	x	_____	= ?

Betty travels to work by bus. The bus costs $1.25 each way. It will cost Betty $2.50 a day to get to and from work. What will her transportation cost be for a month of 22 working days?

Solve It

$2.50 a day	x	Number of days Betty works in a month	=	Monthly cost of transportation

What is the monthly cost?

What Can You Afford for Rent?

The cost of transportation to and from work is one thing to consider. Another thing is your salary. What you earn determines how much you can afford for rent and transportation.

Some people try to keep their rent to 25% of their income. That's not always possible. But it's not a good idea to pay more than 30% of your income for rent. If you pay too much rent, you may not be able to afford other things you need.

You may find an apartment that seems perfect. It's just where you want to live. It's near your work. Your friends live just around the corner. The apartment rents for $390. But 30% of your income is $294. (.30 x $980 = $294) You can't afford to pay $390.

Solve It

$390   rent
−294   what you can afford for rent

How much more would you need?

If your monthly income is $725, what's 30% of your income? Find the answer using your calculator.

Calculator Practice

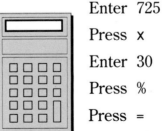

Enter 725

Press x

Enter 30

Press %

Press =

Your answer should be: $217.50

Decide where you want to live. Figure how much you're able to pay. These are the first two steps toward finding your place.

Suppose you've finished with those two steps. What do you do next?

How Do You Find the Place You Need?

There are three ways to begin finding what you want:

Wordwise: A small apartment with no bedroom is called a *studio*.

- Tell people you know about the kind of place you're looking for. Is it a room for rent, an apartment, or a house?
- Go to the neighborhood where you hope to live. Look around. Call to find out about any place that has a *For Rent* sign on it.
- Look in the newspaper. Read the classified **ads** for rooms, apartments, or houses.

When you begin reading the ads, you'll see many **abbreviated** words. Some ads may have very few whole words. Here are three abbreviations often used in housing ads:

AEK	=	all electric kitchen
BR	=	bedroom
BA	=	bathroom

Figuring Out What the Ads Mean

Take a look at the ads on the facing page. Each one has some abbreviated words in it. When you read an ad, you need to know what the abbreviations mean.

Solve It

Work with a partner. Read rental ads 1, 2, and 3 aloud to each other. Use the lists below the ads to decide what some of the abbreviations stand for.

1.	2.	3.
Cute cabin w/view, pvt. sundeck, nr. town. Woodstove. Avail. now. $475. 555-5878	Sm. studio in excel. location. Coin op. laundry on property. $500 mo. incl. all util. Avail. 7/23/90. 1st, sec. & cleaning dep. req'd. Call 555-2458	Very lge. apt., 2 BR, 1 BA, FP. No pets or smoking. $760 mo. 555-5346, 555-4366 mess.

Here is what the abbreviated words mean in ad number 1:

w/: with	nr.: near
pvt.: private	avail.: available (ready to move into)

Here is what the abbreviated words mean in ad number 2:

sm.: small	util.: utilities
excel.: excellent	1st: first month's rent
op.: operated	sec.: security
mo.: month	dep.: deposit
incl.: includes	req'd.: required

Here is what the abbreviated words mean in ad number 3:

lge.: large	FP: fireplace
apt.: apartment	mess.: message (call and leave message)

Look for a complete list of abbreviations in Appendix I in the back of this textbook.

Imagine that you read these three ads. The first one sounds great, but it's too expensive. You know you can't afford it, so you don't bother to call.

1.	2.	3.
APTOS: $745. FP, walk to beach. INCL. ALL UTIL. $945 dep. No last mo. Sorry no dogs. Agent, 555-1866 WESTERN ASSOC. Open 9:30 A.M.–7 P.M./10–2 wknds	CAPITOLA corner Rosedale & Hill. Quiet area. Pool, laundry. 1 & 2 BR, $610 to $740. 850 Rosedale See mgr. / #60 555-2054 or 555-1075	APTOS–1 BR, clean, neat, $575 + dep. Debbie, 555-2066

Here's a Tip: *Incl. All Util.* means all the utilities are included in the cost of the rent.

You're not sure about number 2. It's three miles from your job. But the rents are between $610 and $740. You call and find out that one apartment is not rented. It's $675 a month. To move in, you need to pay first and last months' rent. ($675 + $675 = $1,350) You also need to pay a cleaning **deposit** of $350. ($1,350 + $350 = $1,700)

You don't have this amount of money. So you call and ask about apartment number 3.

You find out that the $575 rent for apartment number 3 includes the cost of utilities. But you have to pay a security deposit in case you damage anything. That's $300. How much money will you need to move in?

Solve It

$575 + $300 = total amount needed to move into apartment number 3

How much do you need?

You decide you can afford this apartment. And it's in a location that suits you. So you go take a look.

You see that the place is very small. But it's comfortable and clean. It may not be perfect, but it will do.

They're Not All the Same: Some apartments will be furnished. Others will have a stove and a refrigerator only. You may need to ask about this when you call. The ad may not tell you.

You talk to the owner, and she gives you a **rental application** to fill out. Here's some of the information the owner may need to have:

1. Your name.
2. The name of anyone else who will be living in the apartment.
3. Where you live now.
4. The address and phone number of the place where you work; how long you've worked there; how much you make.
5. Your roommate's income and place of employment.
6. The name, address, and phone number of someone who knows you and can say you're reliable. (This means a business person who knows you pay your bills. It can be the owner of a place that you have rented before.)

Progress Check 1

1. Write the name, address, and phone number of someone who can say you are reliable about paying your bills.
2. Explain how the person knows you and knows that you pay your bills.

What About Your Deposits? What Happens to Them?

Your rental application is approved and you move in. You have given the owner a money order for $875.

Of that, $300 is your security deposit.

Suppose you live in the apartment for six months. When you leave, you clean everything. But the wall needs repair because you hung something on it that was too heavy. The owner pays $65 to have the wall patched and painted. She subtracts that cost from your security deposit and returns the rest to you.

Solve It

$300 security deposit – $65 for repairs = ?

How much is the **refund** you receive?

Imagine that you leave the apartment, and everything is in good shape. But you lost the second key to the storage locker. The owner subtracts $12 from your deposit for a key.

Solve It

$300 security deposit – $12 for a lost key = ?

How much will you receive back from your security deposit?

Progress Check 2

Write your answers on a separate piece of paper.

1. Vince pays his rent of $575 by the 10th of every month. The first month he paid for 2 months' rent (first and last). He has lived in the apartment from January 10th to June 16th. How much rent has he paid so far? (number of months x the rent = amount of rent paid so far)

Basics Practice

a. $12\overline{)4{,}800}$

b. 25% x $860 =

c. $100.00
    − 89.99

d. $16\overline{)624}$

2. The first apartment Vince called about would have cost him $1,700 to move into. The one he chose cost $875. How much less expensive was it? ($1,700 − $875 = ?)

3. The landlord said Vince could not have more than two people living in the apartment. He is by himself now. How much less would he pay each month if he had a roommate with whom he could split the rent? ($575 ÷ 2 = ? Subtract the answer from $575.)

4. Vince's rent goes up $40 a month. What will the total payment be each month? ($575 + $40 = ?)

What's a Lease For?

A **lease** is a legal contract that usually covers these things:

- how much rent you pay.
- when your rent payment is due.
- the other amounts of money you need to pay, such as a security deposit.
- what things your rent pays for and doesn't pay for.
- the minimum length of time you agree to stay in the apartment.
- what you need to pay if you move before the lease ends.
- when you must tell the owner that you are moving out.

Before you sign a lease, read every part of it carefully. You need to make sure you can agree to everything in the lease.

How a Lease Works

They're Not All the Same: With some leases, you might lose just the last month's rent and security deposit if you move out early. Or you may pay extra rent only as long as the place stays empty.

Suppose you have a lease for your apartment. It says you agree to live in the apartment for at least six months. If you move before that, you're supposed to pay the rent for the remaining months. You pay $425 a month for your apartment. You decide to move two months before your lease runs out.

Solve It

How much will you lose by breaking your lease? ($425 x 2 = ?)

Progress Check 3

Each of the following people is trying to find a place to live. Each person has a different income and a different situation. Read about each one. Then write your answers on a separate piece of paper.

1. Lee and Jack are going to rent a two-bedroom apartment. Lee's monthly income is $625. Jack's is $710. How much can they afford together?

   a. First, multiply Lee's income by .30 (for 30%).

   b. Next, multiply Jack's income by .30 (for 30%).

   c. Now, add the answers you got for a. and b. This shows how much they can afford together.

2. Tim found an apartment that was just what he wanted. The rent was $610 a month. Tim could afford only $560. Tim mentioned the problem to the owner. The owner needed someone to take care of the lawn in front of the apartment. If Tim could do this, he would get a 10% discount on his

rent. Would this lower Tim's rent enough so he could afford it?

a. First, multiply the rent by .10 (for 10%). This tells you how much the discount would be.

b. Next, subtract the discount from the rent. This shows how much rent Tim would pay if he did the lawn work. How much is it?

c. Is your answer less than the $560 Tim can afford to pay for rent?

Calculator Practice

Enter 610

Press x

Enter 10

Press %

Press =

Your discount should be: $61

Enter 610

Press −

Enter the discount.

Press =

Your new rent should be: $549

Basics Practice

a. $247.50
    x   12

b. 30% x $975.00 =

c.   989
    −   92

---

3. Jason wants to rent a room for less than $280 a month. He finds a room in a large house. The rent for the room is $245 a month. Jason will also need to pay his own utilities. They will be about $37 a month.

a. Add the rent and the utilities to find out how much Jason would need to pay out each month. Can he afford the room?

b. How much will Jason have left over, or how much more will he need?

4. Sarah, Lia, and Annette are planning to rent a two-bedroom house. Sarah's monthly income is $1,200. Lia's is $820. Annette's is $780. How much can the three of them afford for monthly rent? Try solving the problem this way:

   a. Add up all three of their monthly incomes.
   b. Multiply that total by .30 (for 30%). How much rent can the three of them afford?
   c. What if each girl decides to spend no more than 25% of her income on rent? How much rent would that be? To answer, multiply each person's monthly income by .25 (for 25%). Then total your three answers.

5. Taylor rents a low-cost room in a hotel. He wants to move into an apartment that will be available in a month. The apartment will rent for $410 a month. Taylor's monthly income is $825. In another month, Taylor will get a 20% raise. How much will he be making then?

   a. First, multiply his monthly income by .20 (for 20%). This shows the amount of the raise.
   b. Next, add the raise to his monthly income. This shows how much he will make in the future.
   c. After getting the raise, will Taylor be able to afford the $410 rent on the apartment? (Multiply his future income by .30.) How much rent will Taylor be able to afford?

Math on the Job

1. Jared Tanapa is the desk clerk at the Stalwart Residential Hotel. Rooms at the hotel rent for $75.00 a week. Rent by the month is $250. Jared explains to a resident that monthly rent is cheaper. He shows him the difference between rent for four weeks and rent for one month. How much less is monthly rent than rent for four weeks?

2. Ralph Saxon takes classified ads on the phone for the daily paper. He has to tell the customer how much each ad will cost. A 3-line ad placed for one day costs $11.66. Every extra word over 3 lines costs 50¢. Ralph is taking a one-day ad with 3 lines and 5 extra words. How much will Ralph charge the customer for the ad?

3. Cruz Herrera is a property manager. She is paid 9% of the monthly rent for each apartment she manages. She gives the owner the rest of the rent after she takes her 9%. She is managing 30 apartments with a total rent of $13,500. How much does Cruz give to the owner each month?

4. May Li is a clerk at the Fair Rent Board in her city. The city does not allow owners to raise rents more than 10% a year. May is talking to a person who rents apartments for $500 a month. How much additional rent can May allow the person to charge for each apartment?

5. Rajid Williams is a real estate agent. Before advertising a house for sale, he figures how much space it has inside. He measures the long wall and the short wall in each room. Then he multiplies the two measurements by each other. That tells him how many square feet of space the room has. The walls in the room he's measuring are 12 feet and 10 feet. How much space does Rajid figure that the room has?

Chapter Review

Chapter Summary

- When you think about finding a place to live, you need to decide on a good location for you. The location should not be too far from your job or school. It should be close to a grocery store and transportation.

- Your rent should not be more than 30% of your income.

- To read a classified rental ad, you need to know many abbreviations. Here are some of the most important ones:

  BR (bedroom)
  BA (bathroom)
  sec. dep. (security deposit)
  1st, Lst (requires first and last months' rent)

- A security deposit pays for anything you damage. The amount of your deposit not used for repairs is refunded to you.

- A lease states the terms for renting the apartment or house.

- Breaking a lease can cost money.

Chapter Quiz

Write your answers on a separate sheet of paper.

1. What does this ad mean?

   Sm 2 BR apt. w/lge sundeck
   close to trans. $580 1st, Lst,
   sec. dep. $300. 555-5555
   mess.

2. You see an apartment that rents for $420 a month. There is a cleaning deposit of $250. What is the total cost to move in?

3. Your salary is $1,100 a month. You don't want to pay more than 30% of your income for rent. How much rent can you afford to pay?

4. You have a lease for 6 months. You move out before the 6 months is up. You paid $480 a month rent and a security deposit of $290. The lease states that if you move early, you must pay one month's rent and lose your security deposit. How much will you need to pay for moving out early?

5. You want to rent a house with two other people. The house rents for $960 a month. How much will each of you pay if you split the rent equally?

6. Your rent is $650 a month. At the end of the year, it is increased by 15%. How much will you pay in January?

Challenge

Think about the kind of apartment you would like to have. It could be any kind of place at all. What would you like it to have inside? How would you want it to look? What about a fireplace, a garden, a sundeck, a garage? Now write the ad for this type of apartment. Use abbreviations like the ones listed in Appendix I in the back of this textbook.

8 Furnishing an Apartment

Buying used furniture can save you a lot of money when you first move out on your own.

Chapter Learning Objectives

- List priorities based on income and need.
- Identify places where large items are sold at low prices.
- Figure cost of items on sale and compare to cash resources available.
- Figure the amount of monthly payments for a layaway plan.
- Figure the amount of monthly payments for a credit account.
- Review basic math skills in the Appendix at the back of this textbook.

Words to Know

appliance   a tool or machine for doing a task, like a vacuum cleaner, washing machine, or can opener

credit application   a form you fill out to get credit so you can buy something now but pay for it later

credit references   people or businesses that can show that you pay your bills and loan payments regularly

down payment   money paid toward the total price of an item

furnishings   furniture, appliances, rugs, curtains, and other items used in a home

layaway plan   a plan in which something is marked sold but is kept in the store until you finish paying for it

priority   coming before something else in order of importance

unpaid balance   amount of money left to pay toward the total price

Starting to Furnish Your Place

Suppose that you've rented an unfurnished or partly furnished place. You find yourself with a bare room or two. So how do you start to furnish them? And where do you start? Most people can't afford to buy everything they need all at once.

Think about the most important **furnishings** that you need for each room. Make a list of what is missing from each room. Write down the item if it's something you really need.

Your needs might include any or all of the following items:

bed frame, mattress, box springs	chairs
refrigerator	chest
sofa	lamps
stove	table

After you've made a list, decide which item you need the most. Mark that number 1. Number the rest of the list to match your needs. You'll have item number 2, number 3, and so on.

As you do this, you're setting priorities. When something has **priority**, it comes before something else in order of importance. A kitchen table, for example, probably has greater priority for you than an end table. When you have set your priorities, you'll know where to begin.

Here's a Tip: The best months to buy furniture are January, February, June, August, and September.

There are two ways to buy the things that are your top priorities:

1. Pay cash.
2. Make time payments. Pay parts of the total amount over a period of time.

Shopping on a Low Budget

Suppose you want to pay cash for the furniture or **appliances** you need most. But you don't have a lot to spend. There are several places where you can find bargains on big items. For example, you might find a low-priced sofa or stove in:

- a used furniture and appliance store.
- a flea market.
- a garage sale.
- the classified ads in the paper.

Solve It

They're Not All the Same: Always look at the back of the furniture you're buying. Check to see if it's wood. Some furniture has heavy cardboard in it. It won't last nearly as long as wood.

1. Imagine that you're looking for a table and a lamp. You find them both at a Saturday garage sale. The table is marked $82.50. The lamp is marked $27.00. How much do the table and lamp cost together? ($82.50 + $27.00 = ?)

2. You have $87.00 to buy both a table and a lamp. How much more do you need if you pay the marked price? (answer to item 1 – $87.00 = ?)

3. You decide to offer less for each item. If you get the lamp for $20 instead of $27, how much will you have left to offer for the table? ($87 – $20 = ?)

When you're buying something at a garage sale or through a classified ad, it often pays to bargain. Try making an offer for less than the asking price, especially if you think the price is too high. The seller might accept your offer or meet your offer halfway.

Progress Check 1

Write your answers on a separate piece of paper.

Did You Know? The average person spends 25 years of his or her life in bed. It makes sense to get a good mattress.

1. At the flea market, you see a bed frame for $33, a mattress for $10, and a box spring for $10. How much do you need to pay to have a whole bed?

2. You find a chest of drawers through a classified ad. The seller wants $100 for it. You offer $75. The seller says "no" to your offer, but agrees to lower the price by $15. If you buy the chest, how much would it cost you?

3. At a garage sale, you see a sofa that looks like new. It costs $95. You need to buy a sofa and a rug for your apartment. You have $117 to spend. You pay $5 off the marked price of the sofa. How much do you have left for the rug?

Imagine that you need a stove. You also want to buy a larger TV. You have $215 in cash to spend on both items. You read about a stove that sounds good in a classified ad. Here's what the ad says:

Cook All Self-cleaning Electric Range. Good condition. Gold, $150. Firm price.

Firm price means the seller will not lower the price.

Solve It

1. Your neighbor has a 21-inch TV for sale at $120. You know you need the stove more than the bigger TV. So you buy the stove for $150. But you still want the TV. How much do you have left to spend on it? ($215 – $150 = amount left for TV)

2. How much more will you need to buy your neighbor's TV? ($120 – amount left for TV = what you'll need for TV)

3. You're in luck. Your neighbor says you can pay $65 now. Then you can pay off the TV in two equal monthly payments. What will you pay for each of the next two months? ($120 – $65 = $55) ($55 ÷ 2 = ?)

Progress Check 2

Write your answers on a separate piece of paper.

1. You decide which things you'll buy first, second, and third. This is called:

   a. setting charges.

   b. setting the clock.

   c. setting priorities.

2. You'll be least likely to find items at a low cost if you look for them at:

   a. flea markets.

   b. garage sales.

   c. new furniture stores.

Wordwise: Sometimes you'll see *wholesale price* on a furniture ad. This is the price the store paid for the item. A store could not make a profit if it sold everything at wholesale prices.

3. You have $95 in cash to buy what you need for your apartment. You need two chairs, a clock, and a bookshelf. You buy two chairs for $30 each. How much do you have left for a clock and a bookshelf? ($30 x 2 = ?) ($95 – amount spent on chairs = amount left for clock and bookshelf)

4. You want to buy a TV described in a classified ad. The seller is asking $165. You have $130 to spend. You ask the seller if she'll take less. She tells you she would take $20 less. Can you buy the TV with your $130?

5. You have $192 to spend on used furniture and appliances. You want to buy a bed at $60, a table and chairs for $45, a chest for $32, and a portable heater for $25. Can you afford all four items? How much more will you need, or how much will be left over?

Using a Layaway Plan

Suppose you need a sofa. You find just what you want in a used furniture store. It's a brown leather sofa. There's a small tear in one of the cushions, but it has been patched. When you turn the cushion over, the tear doesn't show. In fact, then the sofa looks almost new. It costs $352. But you only have $90 in cash! The salesperson suggests that you use a **layaway plan.** This means the store will keep the sofa for you while you make payments on it.

You make a **down payment,** or pay part of the price. Then you make three monthly payments on the **unpaid balance,** or the rest of the money owed. The payments are in equal amounts. After you make the last payment, the sofa is yours. How much will each of the monthly payments be? It depends on the amount of your down payment and the unpaid balance.

Calculator Practice

Use your calculator to figure out four equal payments for the $352 sofa.

Enter 352

Press ÷

Enter 4

Press =

Your down payment should be: $88

Progress Check 3

Write your answers on a separate piece of paper.

1. You want to buy a table that costs $134. You also want to buy a $49 chest for the bedroom. How much will both items cost?

2. You decide to put the table and chest on layaway. You make a down payment of $30. What is the balance due?

3. You pay the balance due in three equal monthly payments. What will each monthly payment be?

Buying Furniture on Credit

You decide to go shopping at a new furniture store. You want to buy a new refrigerator that will last for a long time. You don't want to worry about it needing repair.

You decide to buy your new refrigerator at the Appliance Corral. The model that seems right for your apartment costs $535. You don't have that much cash, so you ask if you can buy it on credit. The salesperson explains how that works.

When you buy on credit, you can have the refrigerator immediately. Then you can take months or years to pay for it. But you'll also pay interest on the money you owe the store. This means you'll pay extra money over the price of the refrigerator. This may be the only way you can afford to buy an expensive item that you need right away.

To buy something on credit, you must first fill out a **credit application**. On the application, you'll answer questions about your income and expenses. This information shows people at the store how much you can afford in monthly payments.

You will be asked to name some **credit references**. Someone will call your references. Be sure to name people or businesses that will speak well of you. They should be people who know that you pay your bills and loan payments regularly.

Progress Check 4

Write your answers on a separate piece of paper.

1. Who would be better to name as a reference on a credit application—the owner of the apartment you rent or your mother? Explain why.

2. Name other credit references you might list on a credit application.

3. Suppose you make $11,000 a year. The credit application has a place for you to show your yearly salary range. Which of these boxes would you need to check?

   ☐ Under $15,000
   ☐ $15–25,000
   ☐ $25–35,000
   ☐ Over $35,000

4. The credit application states: *Previous employer (if under 3 years in present job)*. What name and address would you need to give if you have only been at your present job for a year?

5. You are asked to give the name and address of your bank. Beside the blank, it reads: *Checking? Savings?* Explain what this means.

Here's how Appliance Corral figures the monthly payment for your refrigerator.

Figuring Monthly Payments

$_____		Price	
_____	−	Down Payment	(the part of the price that you pay in cash)
_____	=	Unpaid Balance	(amount you still owe after making a down payment)
_____	+	Interest	(amount charged by the store for money you owe)
_____	=	Total	(total amount of what you will pay for the item)
_____	÷	Number of Months to Pay	
_____	=	Monthly Payment	

Progress Check 5

Copy the shaded side of the Figuring Monthly Payments chart on a separate piece of paper. Then answer the questions below. Fill in each missing amount on your chart.

1. Your refrigerator costs $535. You make a down payment of $35. What is the unpaid balance?
2. Interest on the refrigerator for one year is 20% of the unpaid balance. How much is the total interest?

Calculator Practice

Here's how to use your calculator to answer question 2:

Enter .20

Press x

Enter unpaid balance.

Press =

Your answer should be: $100

---

3. How much is the total cost of a one-year contract? Add the unpaid balance and interest.
4. How much are monthly payments for a one-year credit contract? Divide the answer to question 3 by 12 months.

Shopping for Household Necessities

Suppose you have all your furniture, but there are some smaller items you need. These are necessities that you use regularly.

Here are some sample necessities:

Priority List

✔	vacuum cleaner	✔	a fan
✔	trash bags	____	pots and pans
____	waste basket	✔	a mop
____	towels	____	can opener

The items that are checked are your top priorities. The best places to shop for these items are large variety or discount stores. Their prices will be much lower than those in department stores or specialty shops.

Imagine that you're shopping at Bargains Galore. Here's what the store has on sale today.

---

vacuum cleaner	$77.88	trash bags	$ 3.97
2-pack Flick film	15.37	calculator	16.88
sunglasses	4.20	tire cleaner	1.97
12-pack Fizz-Bubble	3.22	sponge mop	3.97
high-speed fan	39.97	shovel	20.00

Basics Practice

a. $480.00 x .25 =

b. $12\overline{)\$480.00}$

c. $690.00 x .33 =

d.
$$
\begin{array}{r}
45\% \\
13\% \\
+ \ 22\% \\
\hline
\end{array}
$$

Progress Check 6

Write your answers on a separate piece of paper.

1. Look at the Priority List. Which of the items on sale are your top priorities?
2. What will their total cost be?

The examples in this chapter show several ways to buy what you need. If you don't have enough cash, you can use a layaway plan. Or you can buy on credit. The way you pay depends on your income. It also depends on how soon you need something.

For example, you may need a bed right away. Buying it on layaway may take too much time.

Progress Check 7

Write your answers on a separate piece of paper.

1. You're buying things you need for the kitchen. First, you buy a broom that is on sale for $3.77. It's regularly priced at $6.87. How much do you save?

2. Dish detergent is regularly $1.17. Today it's 84¢. How much do you save on two bottles?

3. What are your total savings on the broom and detergent?

4. You find two things you need at a thrift shop—a chest for $67 and a sofa bed for $180. You make a down payment of $40 and put both things on layaway for four months. How much will each of your four equal payments be for the unpaid balance? ($67 + $180 = total cost) (Total cost − $40 = unpaid balance) (Unpaid balance ÷ 4 = monthly payment)

Basics Practice

a. $5.29
    − 1.67

b.   4$\overline{)\$124.00}$

c. $13.50
     39.99
   + 182.13

d. $129.00
    − 57.00

Math on the Job

1. Stacey Thornapple manages a thrift shop. She has to rent more storage space for the furniture she's getting. She'll have to raise prices 3% to cover the cost of the rent. Stacey has a sofa for sale at $250. After she adds 3%, what will the price be?

2. Tyrone Adams is the manager at a flea market. Each seller pays $12.50 for a rental space. Today there were 180 sellers. How much did Tyrone collect for rental space?

Chapter Review

Chapter Summary

- When you need furniture or appliances for an unfurnished place, it helps to set priorities. Then you know what to buy first.

- There are two ways to buy furnishings: pay cash and make time payments.

- To save money, you might shop for furnishings at a used furniture and appliance store. You can also find bargains at flea markets and garage sales, or through classified ads in the paper.

- It is possible to use a layaway plan for a large item. This allows you to buy what you need by making payments for a few months. The store keeps the item until you have made all the payments.

- With a credit account, you can take months or years to pay. You may take home the item immediately.

- To open a credit account, you must fill out a credit application. Then people at the store decide whether you can afford credit payments and are a good credit risk.

- Household necessities are items you use at home regularly. Large variety or discount stores usually offer the lowest prices for such items.

Chapter Quiz

Write your answers on a separate sheet of paper.

1. Name four places where you can find good bargains on large items.

2. You have $156 to spend on furniture. You have no bed, no table, and no chairs. You buy a bed for $65. How much do you have left for your table and chairs?

3. You put a chest and a coffee table on layaway. The chest is $99 and the coffee table is $75. You make a down payment of $35. Then you make four equal monthly payments. How much is each monthly payment?

4. You want to open a credit account at a furniture or appliance store. What main things will the credit people want to know about you?

5. You buy a stove for $399. You pay for it on credit on a one-year contract. You make a down payment of $70. The interest rate on your account is 19%. What will each monthly payment be? (Use the chart on page 128 to help you figure the answer.)

Challenge

Look in the newspaper. Read at least one advertisement for a used furniture store. Or look in the classified ads. Find the cost of the lowest-priced sofa that is advertised. Then find the cost of the highest-priced sofa that is advertised. Do the same for another item, such as a bed. Then read at least one advertisement for a new furniture store. Compare their prices for the same items. Figure how much difference there is between buying used furniture and new furniture.

Unit Four Review

Answer each item. Look back at Chapters 7 and 8 if you need help.

1. List three things you'll need to consider when choosing where to live.

2. List three ways of finding a suitable place to live.

3. List five abbreviations you are likely to find in a classified ad. Tell what each one stands for.

4. List four things covered by a lease.

5. List at least six items of furniture you will need if you rent an unfurnished apartment.

6. Explain the main difference between buying something on a layaway plan and buying something on credit.

7. List three things you might be asked on a credit application.

8. Make a list of the household items *you* would need if you got an apartment right now. Tell where you think could get those items most cheaply.

9. If you are shopping on a low budget, name 4 places you might look to purchase furniture and appliances.

10. On a credit application, you may be asked to list credit references. What is a credit reference?

Unit Five

Buying and Preparing Food

9   Choosing and Buying Groceries

*A farmer's market is a good place to buy **produce** that's fresh and reasonably priced.*

Chapter Learning Objectives

- Compare prices at different supermarkets.
- Compare prices of food brands.
- List three ways to reduce a food bill.
- Identify five kinds of information on food labels.
- Compare prices of canned, frozen, and fresh foods.
- Review basic math skills in the Appendix at the back of this textbook.

Words to Know

generic without a brand name; not advertised and not colorfully packaged

ingredient one of the parts of a mixture

lb. abbreviation for pound; unit of weight

nutritional value the amount of the proteins, vitamins, and minerals that contribute to good health

oz. abbreviation for ounce; unit of weight

per for each

pkg. abbreviation for package

produce vegetables and fruit

Ways to Save on Groceries

What type of shopping will you do most often? Grocery shopping, of course. And because you will do so much of it, you might as well make it easier on yourself. There are some things you can do to make buying food more interesting and less expensive.

Every day you see ads for food in the newspaper, on TV, and in supermarket windows. How do you know where to shop? When you get to the store, how do you know what to buy?

Here are two ways to start:

1. Compare the prices of the same foods at markets. Choose markets that are fairly close to each other and close to you. It doesn't make sense to compare prices at markets that are far away. If you do, it might take you half a day to get there and back home. You want to save money *and* time.

2. The sales on foods can help you decide what to buy. For example, you may be planning on turkey, but you see that ribs are on sale. You may decide to change your plans to take advantage of the sale.

Solve It

Market A	Market B	Market C
Krunch Cereal $2.29	Krunch Cereal $1.89	Krunch Cereal $2.19

Which market sells Krunch Cereal at the lowest price? How much would you save buying Krunch Cereal there than at each of the other two markets?

Read the food ads on the facing page for Lupo's Market and Valley Value. Compare the prices for the foods that are the same. Ask yourself which market is less expensive. Look to see if the amounts that are advertised are the same. Sometimes an item seems to have a lower price. But that's because it weighs much less.

Take a look at the peanut butter at Lupo's. How many ounces are in the jar? What is the price? What is the price **per** ounce? To find out, you divide the price by the number of ounces like this:

$$\$1.44 \div 18 = \$.08 \text{ per } \textbf{oz.}$$

Lupo's Market	Valley Value

Lupo's Market

1 **LB.** PACKAGE
CHICKEN FRANKS **.99**

PORK ROAST
LEAN EASTERN PORK BUTT.......... **1.79** LB.

SPARERIBS
PRIME BACK RIBS FOR THE BBQ **1.19** LB.

PEANUT BUTTER
18 OZ. JAR, CREAMY OR CHUNKY
1.44

Valley Value

SPARERIBS
LEAN COUNTRY STYLE
OR REGULAR SMALL SIDES
1.99 LB.

PEANUT BUTTER
28 OZ. **2.99**

• SHOULDER BUTT
BONELESS PORK ROAST **1.89** LB.

CHICKEN FRANKS
1 lb. **pkg.**,
Reg. 1.39 **69¢**

Progress Check 1

Write your answers on a separate piece of paper.

1. Find the cost per ounce of Valley Value's peanut butter. Compare it to the cost per ounce of Lupo's peanut butter. Which store offers the better deal?
2. Which store sells each of these items at the lower price?
   a. spareribs   b. chicken franks   c. pork roast
3. Where would you shop—at Lupo's or at Valley Value? Why?

Basics Practice

a. $12\overline{)\$6.24}$

b. $16\overline{)\$3.20}$

c. $\begin{array}{r} \$1.99 \\ -\ 1.82 \end{array}$

Comparing Food Prices at a Market

You can compare stores. And you can also compare prices of different brands at one store. Each food comes in many different brands. Most of them will be in one of these two categories:

1. **nationally advertised brands**: big name brands you see in the paper and on TV.
2. **store brands**: brands put out by the market itself or by a chain, or group of markets.

Suppose that today you're at Lupo's Market. You want to get three items for a camping trip: chili with beans, catsup, and peanuts. See how the brand names can make a difference in price. When you go to get your three items, this is what you find.

Food	Nationally Advertised Brand	Store Brand
catsup	$1.09 per 14-oz. bottle	$.85 per 14-oz. bottle
peanuts	6.99 per 11.5-oz. jar	6.49 per 12-oz. jar
chili with beans	1.35 per 15-oz. can	1.09 per 15-oz. can

Progress Check 2

Write your answers on a separate piece of paper.

1. Which is less expensive in all cases—the nationally advertised brand or the store brand?

2. What is the difference in price between the nationally advertised chili and the store brand chili?

Calculator Practice

Here's how to solve item 2 using your calculator:

Enter 1.35

Press –

Then enter 1.09

Press =

Your savings for one can should be: $.26

3. What is the difference in price between the nationally advertised catsup and the store brand catsup?

4. What is the cost per ounce of the nationally advertised catsup? What is the cost per ounce of the store brand catsup? What is the difference in price per ounce?

5. Will you get as many peanuts in the nationally advertised brand jar as you will in the store brand jar? How do you know? What is the difference in price per ounce?

6. Add it up. How much would you spend buying the nationally advertised brands of catsup, peanuts, and chili?

7. How much would you spend if you bought the store brand items, instead? What's the difference in cost to you?

Watch Out for Those Displays!

The displays at the end of the aisles can be tempting. The display catches your eye because of the arrangement or because of the colors. Sometimes you buy an item even when you don't need it or use it regularly. Today Andy sees barbecue sauce in a big display. The sign says: DIGGER'S BAR-B-Q SAUCE ONLY $1.65 PER 14-OZ. JAR. Then he goes down the aisle and sees his regular barbecue sauce. It costs $1.29 and it's in an 18-oz. jar. Which one is the real bargain?

Shopping Tips

Read these ten tips. Each can save you money on your grocery bills.

1. Check ads and compare prices from store to store.
2. Compare the prices of the same item in one store.
3. Plan your menu to use foods that are on sale. Choose fruits and vegetables in season.
4. Don't go shopping when you're hungry.
5. When the items you use often are on sale, buy more than one.
6. Buy **generic** foods or store brands.
7. Avoid buying snack foods.
8. Watch out for eye-catching displays at ends of aisles. Don't let the attractive arrangements influence you. Compare prices before buying.
9. Buy items like rice or nuts from bulk-food bins or barrels at the store. The exact same food in a package usually costs more. Bag your own rice. Why pay for the package?
10. Watch as your groceries are checked out. Make sure you don't get overcharged.

What Do Snacks Do to Your Food Bill?

Look at the shopping list below. The price for each item is shown. The first five items are snack foods. Usually people eat snacks by the handful. Snacks disappear quickly. But they cost a lot per pound.

potato chips	$1.09	coffee	$4.49
roasted peanuts	1.99	bread	.69
cookies	1.39	lettuce	.39
crackers	1.99	cucumbers, 3 for	.99
snacking squares	2.99	ground beef 1 lb.	1.79
bananas 3 lbs.	1.00	top sirloin 1 lb.	2.59
oranges 5 lbs.	1.00	dry cat food	1.29
potatoes 1 lb.	.39		

Snack foods are not very filling. You could snack on other foods for a lot less money. Think about it. How many potato chips could you eat in one sitting? Could you eat that many bananas or that many slices of bread?

Look at the difference in price between a bag of potato chips and three pounds of bananas or one whole loaf of bread.

Basics Practice

a.
$$\begin{array}{r} \$2.20 \\ .79 \\ + \ 3.01 \\ \hline \end{array}$$

b.
$$\begin{array}{r} \$18.32 \\ - \ 5.76 \\ \hline \end{array}$$

c.
$$\begin{array}{r} .79 \\ \times \ 3 \\ \hline \end{array}$$

d. $.50)\overline{\$1.50}$

Solve It

1. How much would it cost to buy all of the food listed on the shopping list?
2. What is the total price of the snack foods (the first five items on the list)?
3. What percentage of the whole amount would be spent on snacks? (answer to question 2 ÷ answer to question 1 = ? %)
4. Can snacks take up a large percentage of your total food bill?

What Do Labels Tell You?

Labels always tell you the brand of the food. They also list the amount that is in the jar, package, or can. But the label tells you other things. Here are some of them:

ingredients: all of the things that make up the mixture in the can, jar, or package. (The first ingredient listed is the one that is the largest amount. Next comes the ingredient that is second in amount and so on.)

nutritional value: the amounts of proteins, vitamins, and minerals important to your health.

notice of artificial coloring, flavoring, or preservatives: things added to food to change the color, improve the taste, or keep the food from spoiling.

Looking at the front of the label is important. For example, if a label says *beef and gravy,* there will be more beef than gravy. The word that comes first names the food that is in the larger amount.

Solve It

The front of the label says *Gravy and Beef.* Which will be in the larger amount?

U. S. RDA stands for *United States Recommended Daily Allowances.* You will find a list of U. S. RDA's on cans and boxes of food. This list will tell you the percentage this product has of the proteins, vitamins, and minerals you should have each day.

See what you can find out from the parts of these labels marked A, B, and C.

A

16 FL OZ (1 PT) - 473 ML

B

INGREDIENTS: LIGHT TUNA, WATER, VEGETABLE BROTH, SALT, HYDROLYZED PROTEIN (CASEIN)

C

SHAKE BEFORE USING
Refrigerate when opened.
Use by date on the can.
NUTRITION INFORMATION
PER SERVING
SERVING SIZE .... 6 FL OZ. (182 g)
SERVINGS PER CONTAINER 1
CALORIES 40
PROTEIN (GRAMS) 1
CARBOHYDRATE (GRAMS) 9
FAT (GRAMS) 0
SODIUM .... 45 mg/serving

PERCENTAGE OF U.S.
RECOMMENDED DAILY
ALLOWANCES (U.S. RDA)
PROTEIN 2
VITAMIN A 45
VITAMIN C 45
VITAMIN B1 2
DIETARY FIBER .... 1 gram/serving
RIBOFLAVIN 2
NIACIN 6
CALCIUM 2
IRON 4

Progress Check 3

Write your answers on a separate piece of paper.

1. Look at jar label A. How many ounces would be in the jar?
2. Look at can label B. Which ingredient is in the second-largest amount?
3. Look at label C. How many grams of protein are in one serving? How many grams of fat?
4. Look at the U.S. RDA list on label C. The food in this can is high in two important vitamins. Which two vitamins? How can you tell?

What Else Do You Need to Watch For?

Sometimes foods have misleading names. The name of an item may make it seem to be the food you want. But it might not be exactly what you think it is.

Here's an example. Suppose you want to buy fruit juice. There are many juices, juice blends, fruit beverages, and fruit drinks to choose from. How do you know which one to buy? Only the ones that say they are *real fruit juice* are made from juice. They are not a mixture of other things. The mixtures usually have a lot of water in them. And some of them have very little, if any, juice.

Look at these samples from the "juice" shelf at one supermarket. Read each one.

Pineapple Juice Unsweetened
Ingredients: pineapple juice and vitamin C

100% Pure Apple Juice
Ingredients: pure apple juice from concentrate

Cherry Juice
Ingredients: pure cherry juice from concentrate

Orange Mango Fruit Juice Beverage
Ingredients: water, white grape juice concentrate, mango pulp, orange juice concentrate, lemon pulp cells, lemon juice concentrate, natural flavors

100% Fruit Juices, Peach
Ingredients: water, concentrated peach, apple and white grape juices, natural flavors

Progress Check 4

Write your answers on a separate piece of paper.

1. Which ingredient is in the largest amount in the sample labeled *100% Fruit Juices, Peach?*

2. Which ingredient is in the largest amount in the sample labeled *Orange Mango Fruit Juice Beverage?*

3. Write the names from the labels of the real juices. These are the ones that don't have anything else added to them (except a vitamin).

There are other things to look for on labels. Sometimes a food has a certain flavor, but it doesn't have the real ingredient. For example, take a look at these two sets of ingredients for chips that are used for cookies and toppings. Read each one carefully. Can you find the difference?

A. Chocolate-Flavored Chips	B. Semi-Sweet Chocolate Chips
Ingredients: sugar, partially hydrogenated vegetable oil, cocoa, nonfat milk, whey, soy, lecithin and sorbitan emulsifiers, salt, vanillin, and other artificial flavors	Ingredients: semi-sweet chocolate (sugar, chocolate liquor, cocoa butter) with added lecithin emulsifiers, and real vanilla

Progress Check 5

Write your answers on a separate piece of paper.

1. Which package contains real chocolate chips?
2. Which ingredient is in the largest amount in package A? Is there any chocolate in the chips?

Canned, Frozen, or Fresh Food?

There are always some foods that you like more than others. So you buy them often. But do you know the least expensive way to buy your favorite foods? Are they less expensive if they are canned, frozen, or fresh? Take a look at the price differences found in these two vegetables.

	Canned	Frozen	Fresh
Green beans	$ .75 per lb.	$ .79 per 8 oz.	$ .89 per lb.
Asparagus	2.29 per 15 oz.	1.89 per 8 oz.	2.99 per lb.

Here's a Tip: Price is not always the main consideration when you buy food. You may buy fresh vegetables because you think they taste better. You may buy them because they're more nutritious.

Progress Check 6

Write your answers on a separate piece of paper.

1. There are 16 ounces in a pound. Look at the prices for the green beans. How much does a pound of frozen green beans cost? ($ .79 + $ .79 = ?) What is the least expensive way to buy them? Which kind do you think would taste better?

2. Look at the prices for the asparagus. What is the least expensive way to buy asparagus?

3. During harvest season, do you think it costs more or less to buy vegetables fresh? Why?

Math on the Job

1. Hank Little needs to buy snacks for the children in his after-school sports camp. He could buy 12 bags of potato chips at $1.29 each. Or he could buy 6 loaves of bread at $.69 each and a 24-ounce jar of peanut butter for $2.98. Which snack would be cheaper? How much cheaper?

2. Lucille Bradshaw is a checker at Valley Value Supermarket. Accidentally, Lucille rang up a wrong price on her cash register. Instead of $3.90 for hamburger, she entered $39.00. When she subtracts the right price from the mistake, how much will she take off the bill?

3. Estella Ortiz needs 20 ounces of noodles for a dish she will make for her office pot-luck. She could buy exactly 20 ounces of noodles from her market's bulk bin. The bulk price is $.12 per ounce. Or she could buy three 8-ounce packages of noodles on sale for $.79 per package. This would give her some noodles leftover. Which would be the better buy? How much better?

4. Violet Minh runs a catering service from her kitchen. She has budgeted $35.00 for vegetables for the Parent-Teacher buffet. Violet is shopping at Valley Value. She has bought $9.04 worth of carrots, $10.60 of celery, and $7.90 of lettuce. She is about to buy $5.88 worth of radishes. What will she have left for the rest of her vegetable menu?

5. Grocery store manager Dennis O'Rourke is reading the advertising circular from another market. The other market is selling hamburger at $3.49 a pound. The price at Dennis's store is $3.75. Dennis wants his store to compete for customers. If Dennis discounts his hamburger by 8%, will he beat the other market's price?

6. Juan Perez is a stock clerk at Lupo's Market. He is setting up a sale display of Yummy brand catsup and mayonnaise. Yummy catsup is normally priced at $1.09 for a 14-ounce bottle. Yummy mayonnaise regularly sells for $1.28 for a 16-ounce jar. Juan must mark down each item by 12¢. What price should he place on each 14-ounce Yummy catsup bottle? On each 16-ounce Yummy mayonnaise jar?

7. Jeff and Linda are having a dinner party Saturday night. At the market, Linda can buy a 20 pound turkey for $35.80 or a 15 pound roast for $28.35. Which item would be the better buy?

8. Linda needs carrots for a salad. She sees one bunch at $.98 for 2 pounds. Loose carrots sell for $.40 for 1 pound. Which carrots are the better buy?

Chapter Review

Chapter Summary

- It pays to compare prices at stores and to compare prices of various food brands.

- Nationally advertised brands will cost more than store brands or generic foods.

- Displays can catch your eye. But they won't necessarily offer you a bargain.

- Buying snacks can add quite a lot to your food bill.

- Labels give you information about the foods you buy. They tell about the brand, the food, the amount, and the ingredients.

- Labels also give information about nutritional value. They list any artificial coloring, flavoring, or preservatives used.

- Sometimes the name of an item can fool you. The food may not really be what you think it is. It is important to read the labels to know what you're buying.

- There are big price differences among canned, fresh, and frozen foods. It is a good idea to compare them.

Chapter Quiz

Write your answers on a separate sheet of paper.

1. You're buying a package of pasta. What should you consider when you compare it to another package?

2. Which of these would have the lowest price?

    a. nationally advertised brands

    b. store brands

    c. generic foods

3. You buy some detergent that is in an 11.5-ounce bottle. It costs $2.99. Another bottle costs $2.49 and holds 12 ounces. What is the cost per ounce of the one you bought? What is the cost per ounce of the one you didn't buy? What is the difference in cost per ounce?

4. When an item is in a display, it is

    a. always a good buy.

    b. sometimes a good buy.

    c. spoiled.

5. If you bought a three-pound turkey breast at $1.89 per pound, how much would you spend?

6. Which can has the less expensive coffee: a 26-ounce can at $6.59 or a 13-ounce can at $2.99?

7. You see applesauce on sale in a display at $1.29 for a 44-ounce jar. Back on the shelf, another brand that comes in the same-size jar sells for $1.09. How much would you lose by buying two jars from the display?

Challenge

Make out a shopping list of foods you would like to eat. Then scan the food section of the paper to find the price for each thing. Write down the prices next to the items. Add up your total bill. Now go through your list and cross out everything that is a snack, soft drink, or extra item you don't need. Add up the prices of everything you crossed out. What percentage of your total food bill was made up of unnecessary foods?

10 Eating for Good Health

Preparing healthful meals is an important part of living on your own.

Chapter Learning Objectives

- Interpret charts and tables that give information about food groups, protein intake, and calories.
- Identify foods that make up a balanced **diet**.
- Figure protein requirements for a person based on age and weight.
- Calculate calories consumed and calories burned.
- List at least two differences between healthful and unhealthful food preparation.
- Review basic math skills in the Appendix at the back of this textbook.

Words to Know

calorie   unit of energy supplied by food

cholesterol   a waxy substance in animal fats

diet   the food and drink that is consumed by a person

gram   a unit of weight in the metric system; about twenty-eight grams equal one ounce

nutritious   nourishing; valuable as food

protein   a substance that is a necessary part of the cells of animals and plants

saturated fat   lard, suet, butterfat, chicken fat, and others that stay solid at room temperature

unsaturated fat   oils like olive oil, corn oil, safflower oil, and others that are liquid at room temperature

What Kinds of Foods Do You Really Need?

There are certain kinds and amounts of foods that people need every day. Those foods come from five food groups.

1. meat, poultry, fish
2. milk, yogurt, cheese
3. vegetables
4. bread, cereals, rice, pasta
5. fruits

The right amount of foods from these groups makes up a balanced diet. And when you have a balanced diet, you're getting proper nutrition.

Take a look at the chart on the next page.

The chart shows the kinds and amounts of foods a person needs regularly.

Foods Required for Good Nutrition

Fruit Group	Milk Group	Meat Group	Vegetable Group	Bread and Cereal Group
2–4 servings daily of whole fruit, raw or canned fruit or unsweetened fruit juice	2–3 servings *9–12 yr.-olds:* 3 or more cups daily *teenagers:* 4 or more cups daily *adults:* 2 or more cups daily (Cheese, ice cream, and yogurt can help fulfill these requirements.)	2–3 servings 5–7 ounces a day of beef, veal, pork, lamb, poultry, fish, shellfish, or eggs *or* dried beans, peas, nuts, or peanut butter	3–5 servings of a dark green or deep yellow vegetable at least every other day; citrus fruit or other fruit or vegetable rich in vitamin C; other fruits and vegetables, including potatoes	6–11 servings a day of breads (whole grain or enriched), rolls, cereals, crackers, macaroni, spaghetti, noodles, rice, or grits

Progress Check 1

Measurement Table

2 cups = 1 pint

2 pints = 1 quart

2 quarts = one half gallon (8 cups)

2 half gallons = one gallon (16 cups)

Write your answers on a separate piece of paper.

1. At what age does a person require the most milk? If you were going to buy milk for six teenagers for one day, how much would you need? Look at the Foods Required for Good Nutrition chart. Then figure your answer. (6 teenagers x 4 cups = ? cups) Look at the measurement table on the left. Give your answer in the largest amount.

2. How much milk would you buy for two nine-year-old girls for one day?

3. In a seven-day period, how many servings from the bread group should a person have?

4. In a seven-day period, how many servings from the meat group should a person have?

5. What can you eat from the meat group that is *not* meat? List those things.

6. Which food group allows the largest number of servings daily?

7. In a seven day period, how many servings from the fruit group should an adult have?

8. Which group should you have the smallest amount of daily?

9. What is the total number of servings an adult should have daily from all the groups combined?

10. In a seven day period, how many servings from the vegetable group should an adult have?

Before you shop, it's a good idea to go over your grocery list. See how many of the foods you have chosen are ones that your body needs every day. Also, when you eat in restaurants, order foods that are **nutritious**.

Look at the Foods Required for Good Nutrition chart. Do you eat enough food from each group every day?

Think about this list when you shop for groceries.

Progress Check 2

Write your answers on a separate piece of paper.

1. Write down everything you ate yesterday. Beside each item, name its food group. Put a question mark beside each item you cannot classify by food group.
2. Look back at the Foods Required for Good Nutrition chart. Compare what it says to what you ate yesterday. Did you eat enough from each food group to give you a balanced diet? If not, what might you eat today to make up for food groups you missed yesterday?

Best Foods for Health

A group of people interested in nutrition studied foods. Here are the foods in each group that are known to be the most nutritious. Take a look. Some of them may be ones you've never eaten!

Sample High-nutrition Foods from Each Food Group

Top Fruits	Top Vegetables	Top Meats	Top Milk Products	Top Breads and Cereals
cantaloupe	frozen collard	beef liver	skim milk	whole wheat
watermelon	greens	chicken liver	buttermilk	bread
oranges	kale	liver sausage	low-fat yogurt	pumpernickel
strawberries	frozen broccoli	chicken breast	Swiss cheese	bread
grapefruit	turnip greens	tuna	whole milk	brown rice
bananas	spinach			enriched
				pasta

Progress Check 3

Write your answers on a separate piece of paper.

They're Not All the Same: Nutrition needs are different for different people. Your food needs vary, depending on your age, weight, and activity level.

1. Which food group has the largest number of sample food choices?
2. Look at the chart. Choose foods you could have for breakfast. Then do the same for lunch and dinner. Make up separate menus for breakfast, lunch, and dinner. Next to each food on your menus, write the food group it comes from.

The foods that make up proper nutrition will have **protein**, vitamins, minerals, starch, fiber, natural sugar, and **unsaturated fat.** The required amounts are measured in **grams.**

This table helps you to find out the amount of protein you need. For example, suppose you're 17 years old and you weigh 148 pounds. Find your age at the left. Then multiply your weight by the grams of protein per pound. The answer will be the amount of protein you need every day. (148 lbs. x .39 grams of protein = 62 grams you need every day)

Your Age	Your Weight		Grams of Protein per Pound		
11–14 years	_____	x	0.45	=	—
15–18 years	_____	x	0.39	=	—
19 and over	_____	x	0.36	=	—

Progress Check 4

Write your answers on a separate piece of paper.

1. Use the information from the chart. Find your protein requirement for the day.

2. Suppose today you had foods containing the following grams of protein:

> 1 egg   5.9
> 1 glass milk   8.45
> 1/2 lb. hamburger   43.2
> 1 serving pot roast   35
> 1 oz. peanut butter   4.5

How much more or less would you need to fill your protein requirement for the day?

Counting Calories

A little over a century ago, men consumed 6,000 to 6,500 **calories** a day. Women consumed 4,000 to 4,500. Now men and women consume less than half those amounts. But, most people are consuming more calories than their bodies use.

Different kinds of foods have different numbers of calories. Take a look at this sample of foods. The amount and number of calories are shown for each food.

Wordwise: When you consume something, you use it up. In this chapter, *consume* means to use up something by drinking or eating it.

Food	Amount	Calories
apple	1 small	64
bacon	1 1/2 slices	53
string beans	3/4 cup	43
lean beef	1 slice	190
white roll	1 large	100
butter	2 teaspoons	77
chocolate cake	1 slice	200
chicken	4 oz.	125
corn on the cob	1 medium	90
cucumber	1 medium	15
egg	1 whole	75

Food	Amount	Calories
frankfurters	2	244
grapefruit	1/2 medium	36
lettuce	10 leaves	10
baked potato	1 medium	92
pork chop	4 oz.	240
tomato	1 medium	20
soda crackers	2 large	53

Progress Check 5

1. Ruth had these foods for dinner: a salad with lettuce (10 leaves), 1 medium tomato, and 1/2 a cucumber. She also had 3/4 cup of string beans and a baked potato with four teaspoons of butter on it. In addition, Ruth had two slices of lean roast beef. For dessert, she had a piece of chocolate cake. How many calories did Ruth have for dinner? Write down the foods and add up the calories on a separate piece of paper.

2. Choose your five favorite foods from the chart. Write down each one. Next to it, write the number of calories it has. Which of your favorite foods has the highest number of calories?

Burning Calories with Exercise

The number of calories you use during the day depends on what you do. If you take in more calories than you need, you gain weight. But you can exercise to burn up extra calories. The table on the next page shows how much exercise burns up a certain number of calories.

Activity	Calories Used Per Hour
sitting	72–84
standing	120–150
walking (2 miles per hour)	150–240
bowling, cycling (6 miles per hour)	240–300
digging in garden	360–420
shoveling snow	420–480
sawing wood, playing touch football	480–460
running (5 1/2 miles per hour)	600–660

Progress Check 6

Write your answers on a separate piece of paper.

1. What is the highest number of calories you could burn while sitting for two hours?

2. Compare the highest number of calories for sitting and standing. Find out how many more calories you can use in an hour of standing.

3. You shoveled snow for half an hour. What is the highest number of calories you could have burned?

4. You played touch football for one and a half hours. What is the highest number of calories you could have used?

Too Much of a Good Thing?

Too much fat, sugar, and salt are not at all healthful. Sugar, salt, and fats may make foods taste good. But they don't do good things for your health.

The average American consumes eight times the amount of fat that he or she needs daily. The extra fat is as much as one whole stick of butter.

Fat is more fattening than starch or sugar. Fat has nine calories per gram. Starch and sugar each have four calories per gram.

Solve It

How many more calories are in 25 grams of fat than in 25 grams of sugar?

> 25 x 9 = ?
>
> 25 x 4 = ?
>
> calories of fat – calories of sugar = ?

Which Fat Is Fatter?

All animal fats contain **cholesterol**. People who eat large amounts of animal fats are more likely than other people to have heart disease and other health problems.

Saturated fats include lard, butter, beef fat, and chicken fat. They all increase cholesterol in the blood.

Unsaturated fats are mostly vegetable oils. They don't add to the amount of cholesterol in a person's blood.

Fried foods often have a lot of fat, and they may be hard to digest. It is a good idea to avoid fried food. Eat baked, boiled, stewed, broiled, and barbecued foods, instead.

Sugar Facts

1. Sugar provides none of the 44 nutrients a person needs.
2. The average person eats an average of 120 pounds of sugar a year.

3. The nutritional value of different kinds of sugar is the same. White sugar, brown sugar, honey, raw sugar, or fructose (sugar from fruit) all affect your body in the same way.

4. Sugar uses up vitamins and minerals in your body.

5. Your blood sugar drops within an hour of eating a sweet snack by itself. Then you may feel more tired or hungry.

6. One-fourth to one-fifth of the calories you eat each day comes from sugars that are added to foods.

7. Some sweetened cereals contain 40% to 60% sugar. You may get four teaspoons of sugar in a one-ounce bowl of cereal.

8. Bran cereals often contain higher amounts of sugar than other cereals.

What Kind of Choices Will You Make?

When you make choices about what you'll eat, do yourself a favor. Choose the food that's best for you.

Progress Check 7

Write your choices on a separate piece of paper. Next to each choice, tell why you didn't choose the other item in each pair.

What if you had to choose between these pairs of foods? Which ones would you pick for good nutrition?

1. a. a serving of frozen peas with butter added
   b. fresh peas with unsaturated margarine

2. a. plain cereal with fresh fruit
   b. cereal coated with sugar

3. a. fresh chicken thighs
    b. packaged fried chicken

Why Cut Down on Salt?

How much salt do you eat in a year? Most people eat about 15 pounds. This salt can be very bad for your health.

Calculator Practice

Suppose you eat 15 pounds of salt in a year. How many ounces do you eat in a month? (There are 16 ounces in one pound. There are 12 months in a year.)

Enter 16

Press **x**

Enter 15

Press ÷

Enter 12 and press =

Your answer should be: 20

The recommended amount of salt is $\frac{1}{2}$ to $1\frac{1}{2}$ teaspoons a day. But the average person eats 2 to 4 teaspoons of salt a day.

Solve It

In one day, how much of the salt you eat isn't needed?

$$4 \text{ teaspoons (renamed)} = 3\frac{2}{2}$$
$$- 1\frac{1}{2} \text{ teaspoons} \qquad\qquad - 1\frac{1}{2}$$

About one-third of the salt we eat comes naturally from dairy products, meats, and fish. Another third is added to foods before they're sold. Canned soup is an example. One can of soup may contain all the salt you should consume in one whole day. The other one-third of the salt you eat comes from your salt shaker.

Progress Check 8

Write your answers on a separate piece of paper.

1. Which has the highest amount of calories?

   a. fat   b. sugar   c. starch

2. How many of our required nutrients are provided by sugar?

   a. 44   b. 10   c. none

3. How much sugar does the average person consume in a year?

   a. 10 pounds   b. 100 tablespoons   c. 120 pounds

4. Which is the most healthful way to cook meat?

   a. fry it   b. bake it in butter   c. bake, broil, or barbecue it

5. One large white roll has 100 calories. Two teaspoons of butter have 77 calories. At dinner you had two rolls with two teaspoons of butter on each one. How many calories did you eat in rolls and butter alone?

6. After dinner, you watched TV for three hours. While you sat, you used 84 calories an hour. How many calories did you burn? Did you use up the calories from the rolls and butter?

Basics Practice

a. $120 \div 12 = ?$

b. $1\frac{1}{2}$
     $+ \frac{1}{2}$
     _____

c. $4 \times 92 =$

d. $1\frac{1}{3}$
     $+ \frac{1}{3}$
     _____

What's Wrong with This Menu?

french fries
chicken fried steak and pan gravy
dinner rolls and butter
two soft drinks

Does this menu provide a balanced diet? No, it doesn't. Why? It doesn't include foods from each of the five food groups. It is also high in fat, salt, and sugar. Think about how you could change it.

Progress Check 9

Write your answers on a separate piece of paper.

1. Rewrite the menu so it shows a balanced diet. Use items from this list.

margarine	canned soup
peaches	fresh green beans
lettuce	milk
tomatoes	chocolate cake
rice	ice cream
cucumber	donuts
fresh peas	chicken breast

2. Judith wants to stick to 2,000 calories a day. At breakfast, she had 300 calories. At lunch, she ate 615. How many calories can she have at dinner?

3. Raymond consumed 150 calories at breakfast, 350 at lunch, and 1,200 at dinner. He is going running tonight. Running for one hour would burn up 660 calories. But Raymond will run for only half an hour. How many calories will he burn? Total the number of calories Raymond ate. What percentage of the total will Raymond burn by running?

Math on the Job

1. Jimmy Riles is a clerk at Big Bob's Sporting Goods Store. A customer asks Jimmy how many calories she'll burn while running. The woman wants to run three hours a day. Jimmy knows that running burns 660 calories an hour. How many calories does Jimmy tell the woman she'll burn?

2. Dee Markham works at Valley Hospital. She plans patients' meals. Valley Hospital serves breakfast to 208 patients a day. Dee always plans a menu that includes $\frac{1}{2}$ cup of juice per patient. How many gallons of juice must she order for a two-week supply? (There are 16 cups to a gallon; there are seven days in a week.)

3. Michael Mehta is a commercial artist. He makes posters for a health club. The poster he is drawing tells about protein in popular foods. Michael is figuring the right number of grams of protein in peanut butter. He knows that a 16-oz. jar contains 72 grams of protein. How many grams will he put in his drawing of a one-ounce serving?

4. Doris Ulmoe plans school lunches. She has to keep track of how many calories the lunches contain. Today's menu includes:

   - a broiled pork chop at 240 calories.
   - steamed string beans at 43 calories.
   - steamed rice at 117 calories.
   - a large white roll at 100 calories.
   - butter (2 teaspoons) at 77 calories.

   How much will Doris write down for this meal?

5. Doris needs to decide on dessert. Which of these could she add to the menu so that lunch is no more than 700 calories? Write the letters of each correct answer.

   a. $\frac{1}{2}$ cup of fruit cocktail at 95 calories

   b. 1 slice of chocolate cake at 200 calories

   c. 1 medium apple at 80 calories

   d. 1 cup of whole milk, vanilla yogurt at 140 calories

   e. 1 medium banana at 85 calories

   f. 1 cup vanilla ice cream at 270 calories

6. Carmen Maggio is a butcher. She is making a chart to help people choose meat that is low in cholesterol. Cholesterol is measured in milligrams. (A *milligram* is one-thousandth of a gram.) She will list 3-ounce servings of each of these meats: lean beef (73 milligrams), dark-meat chicken (78 milligrams), shrimp (86 milligrams), and veal (84 milligrams). She will list the meats in order, starting with those with the most milligrams of cholesterol. Make a list to show what Carmen's chart will look like.

7. How many more milligrams of cholesterol are in dark-meat chicken than lean beef?

8. How many more milligrams of cholesterol are in shrimp than in veal?

9. Mrs. Wallace is a high-school teacher. She has asked her students to multiply their weight by 0.39 to determine how many grams of protein they need every day. Which students made a mistake in their figuring? What correct answer will Mrs. Wallace write on the paper for each of those students?

   a. Will, who weighs 200 pounds, wrote .79 grams.

   b. Caroline, who weighs 125 pounds, wrote 48.75 grams.

   c. Ralph, who weighs 175 pounds, wrote 6,825 grams.

   d. Juanita, who weighs 105 pounds, wrote .49 grams.

   e. Chuck, who weighs 182 pounds, wrote 70.98 grams.

Chapter Review

Chapter Summary

- There are certain kinds and amounts of foods that people need every day. These foods come from five food groups.
  - meat, poultry, fish
  - vegetables
  - milk, yogurt, cheese
  - breads, cereals, rice, pasta
  - fruits

- Foods that make up proper nutrition provide protein, vitamins, minerals, starch, fiber, natural sugar, and unsaturated fat.

- Different kinds of foods have different amounts of calories. Most people take in more calories than they use.

- Different kinds of exercise use up different numbers of calories.

- Too much fat, sugar, and salt are not good for your health. Cholesterol, which is found in fat, can build up in your blood and lead to serious health problems.

- You can make choices about what you eat and how it is prepared. These choices will make a difference in your health.

Chapter Quiz

Write your answers on a separate sheet of paper.

1. Who requires more milk in a day—a 9- to 12-year-old, a teenager, or an adult?

2. Patty went for a walk and burned 240 calories. Then she came home and ate a piece of apple pie, which had 274 calories. How many more calories did Patty take in than burn up?

3. A person 11 to 14 years old needs .45 grams of protein per pound of weight. Your 13-year-old brother weighs 110 pounds. How many grams of protein does he need in a day?

4. Name the four food groups.

5. For breakfast, Joanne scrambled two eggs in 4 teaspoons of butter. An egg has 75 calories. Two teaspoons of butter have 77 calories. How many calories were in this part of her meal?

6. One glass of milk has 8.45 grams of protein. Donald had three glasses of milk. How much protein did he consume?

7. What's the difference between saturated and unsaturated fat? Which is the best kind of fat to eat and why?

8. Alma eats about 4 teaspoons of salt every day. A person needs $1\frac{1}{2}$ teaspoons a day at the most. In a week, how much salt does Alma eat that her body doesn't need?

Challenge

Ask a local restaurant for a menu you can keep. (Use a take-out menu, if necessary.) Cross out all the items that have a lot of fat, salt, or sugar. See what remains on the menu.

Now make up your own menu. Put the name of your restaurant or cafe at the top of the paper. Choose what you'll serve for breakfast, lunch, and dinner. Include foods from the four food groups. Make sure you don't have a lot of fatty, sweet, or salty foods. Add a price for each item.

When you're done, compare your menu with those of your classmates. See which menu sounds the most appealing. Where would you want to eat tonight? At which restaurant would the food be least expensive?

Unit Five Review

Write the numbers 1 to 5 on a separate sheet of paper. Read the questions. Choose the best answer. Then write the letter next to its number. Look back at Chapters 9 and 10 if you need help.

1. What is a generic food?

    a. a food with no brand name and no fancy packaging
    b. a nationally advertised brand
    c. a private brand

2. Is price the only thing to consider when you buy food?

    a. Yes. You want to make sure you stick to your budget.
    b. No. You want to buy foods that are nutritious and tasty.
    c. No. You want to buy the most convenient foods.

3. What kinds of foods do you need for proper nutrition?

    a. foods from the meat, milk, and bread/cereal groups
    b. foods from the vegetable and fruit groups
    c. all of the above

4. What is a calorie?

    a. a food that is good for you
    b. a unit of energy supplied by food
    c. a kind of cholesterol

5. Which of these meals would be the most healthful?

    a. a burger, fries, and a shake from Hamburger Haven
    b. fried chicken, buttered mashed potatoes, and pie
    c. green beans, broiled fish, baked potato, and fruit salad

Unit Six

Buying Personal Items

11 Deciding What You Need

Is something you need on sale? How can a newspaper help you find it?

Chapter Learning Objectives

- Name the three important considerations to use in planning personal spending.
- Identify the costs of overlooking health care.
- Use lifestyle and daily activities in deciding which personal items it makes sense to buy.
- Compare quality, quantity, and size of items listed in ads.
- Name ways in which ads may be misleading.
- Review basic math skills in the Appendix at the back of this textbook.

Words to Know

appearance   the way something looks

asterisk   a star-shaped symbol (*) used to refer to a special note on a printed page

markup   the difference between the wholesale, or store's, price and the price the store charges the customer

prescription   a doctor's direction or order for preparing and using medicine

quality   how good something is

retail   the price stores charge the customer

wholesale   the price a store pays for an item

Buying on the Spot

Have you ever gone shopping for some socks you needed and come home with a fancy sweater instead? The sweater looked great. So you bought it on the spot. What does *buying it on the spot* mean? It means seeing something you like and buying it without thinking if you can afford it or need it.

This kind of buying is fine, if you do it only once in a while. But if you do it regularly, you won't have any money left for things you really need.

If you shop carefully most of the time, you'll be able to put money aside for the things you want.

What Do You Really Need?

Figure out what you really need first. Keep in mind three important parts of your life.

1. your health
2. your **appearance**
3. the way you spend your time

These are the parts of your life that you need to take care of. How you feel, how you look, and what you do are all important to a healthy life.

Personal Spending for Good Health

Think about your health. If you don't keep yourself in good health, you won't enjoy the rest of your life. Ask yourself these questions about your health care.

Health Inventory Check

- Are there any **prescription** medicines that I need to take?
- Do I go to a dentist to have my teeth cleaned every six months and checked once a year?
- Do I see a doctor if I'm sick or injured?
- What am I doing to keep in good shape?

They're Not All the Same: Do you have health insurance on the job? If so, find out what your health plan covers. Some just pay for large medical or hospital bills. But some pay for dental bills, too, even the bills for regular check-ups.

These are some of the most important things you'll spend your money on. They come first. It's a good idea to save for the things listed above. (Even if you have health insurance, it won't pay for all of these things.)

Progress Check 1

Write your answers on a separate piece of paper.

1. Jackie puts aside $250 a year to take care of her teeth. Twice a year she gets a checkup and has her teeth cleaned. The checkup costs $35 and the cleaning $42. How much does she spend on her teeth in one year?

2. Does Jackie have any money left over from the $250 she put aside for regular dental care? Why do you think Jackie decided to put aside that extra money?

3. Arlo didn't save anything for dental care. He lost a filling. Having the filling replaced would have cost $80. He didn't go to the dentist. His tooth split. He had to have it capped. That cost $400. How much would Arlo have saved by getting the filling fixed in the first place?

4. Lia needs a prescription for an allergy. It costs $15 a month to have the prescription filled. Lia decides not to have it filled this month. She spends the $15 on a new purse. Then she has a bad allergy attack. She misses work for two days and loses $128 from her pay. Counting the loss in pay, what did the new purse cost her?

Spending Money on Clothes You Need

Here's a Tip: If you can wear the same clothes for work, school, and going out, you'll save money. If you can get shoes that'll be right to wear all the places you go, you'll save again.

What you do determines what you need to wear. Do you go to school? Do you go to work? Do you dress up to go out? Think about where you go and what you do most of the time. Clothes for these activities are the ones you'll need to buy first. Then think about what you do the other hours of the day. Clothes for these activities are the ones you'll need next.

Here's the way Brett's week worked out.

Solve It

Brett spends 30 hours a week at school
7 hours with friends on a weekend
15 hours a week at part-time work

What kind of clothes would Brett buy first—clothes for school, job, or fun clothes?

What kind would come second?

When you shop for clothes, make a list. Stick to it. Otherwise, you might spend money on clothes you don't need or wear.

It's important to think about the weather, too. You wouldn't want to wear a sweater to work when it's 92 degrees outside. Neither would you go without a coat or jacket on a cold day.

Progress Check 2

Read the advertisement below to find the answers. Write your answers on a separate piece of paper.

Easy-to-wash, no-iron
Blouses   each **$13.99**

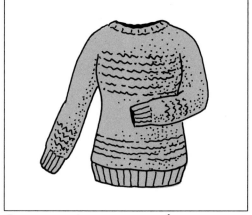

Fashionable Cotton-knit   **each**
Women's Sweaters!   **only** **$13.99**

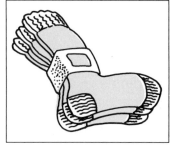

Cotton socks for men on-the-job
3 pairs per pkg **NOW ONLY**
(reg. $3.87)   **$2.88** Pkg.

Men's
Wash 'n Wear
Knit Shirts
on sale for
13.88 each
(regularly priced
at $17.99)

1. Ed just started back to school. He also works 15 hours a week. He has two shirts that he can wear to school. He has plenty of work clothes, except for socks. He buys two more shirts and two packages of socks. How much does he spend?

2. Laura was looking for summer blouses. She bought one blouse and two sweaters. How much did she spend? It's hot in the summer. Did she buy clothes that matched her summer needs?

Tips for Dressing on the Job

1. Notice what other people are wearing at your work. What kind of shoes do most of them wear? (Boots, work shoes, tennis shoes, or leather shoes? High heels, medium heels, or flats?)

2. Notice what your boss wears. When you're making clothes choices, consider what your boss thinks is appropriate.

Did You Know?
If you buy clothes out-of-season, you can often get a better price. Clothes for summer will be on sale as summer ends. Clothes for winter will be on sale as winter ends.

3. Buy clothes that'll last a long time. It's better to have a few good quality clothes than many clothes that'll wear out soon.

4. Get clothes that are comfortable. Can you sit, bend, and stretch in your clothes? Think about the temperature where you work. Is there air conditioning? Is there heat where you work? Are you outside a lot?

5. If possible, try to get clothes you can wear other places, too. Can you wear your work clothes on a date? To school? To other places you go often?

6. Read the clothing labels before you buy. Does the label say that the item must be dry-cleaned only? Dry-cleaning bills can add up. You can save money by buying clothes that you can wash yourself.

Progress Check 3

Write your answers on a separate piece of paper.

1. Tom was choosing clothes to wear for his job
   interviews at department stores. These are clothes
   that he liked:

a red shirt	$40.00
a long-sleeved, blue dress shirt	19.00
a brown leather jacket	225.00
white jeans	58.00
gray slacks	42.00
a dark gray belt	16.00

   How much would Tom spend if he bought all
   these clothes?

Calculator Practice

How much would all the items cost? Add
the prices on the calculator.

What percentage of the total is the price
of the red shirt?

Enter 40

Press ÷

Enter total price of all items.

Press =

Your answer should be: .10 or 10%

2. Tom bought the blue dress shirt, the belt, and the
   gray slacks. He found a good gray jacket at a thrift
   store for $30. How much did Tom spend for his
   interview clothes?

3. Tom's friend, Sid, came with him. Sid was going for a
   weekend to the beach. He bought the white jeans and
   the red shirt for his trip. How much did Sid spend?

Other Expenses for Good Appearance

When you think about how you want to look, you probably think about clothes first. Then you think about what else you need to look good. Here are some of the things you'll need to take care of.

- your hair
- your teeth
- your nails
- your skin

Look at the products in these ads. Which ones could be used to keep up personal appearance?

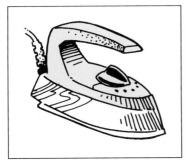

Specially priced $17.99
our $22.99 STEAM-EASY IRON takes the wrinkles out of your day

$2ea. **Creamy**
in 18-oz. **Skin Lotion**
bonus size, easy-squeeze bottles. (limit: 2 per customer)

SALE PRICE! $27.97
Sunny Tone AM/FM clock radio with cassette player and battery backup

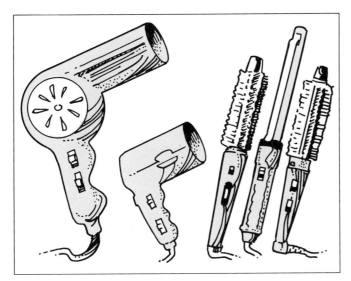

**GET SET
with these FAIR-AIR
Bonus Buys!**

FAIR-AIR
1500-Watt Hair Dryer or

FAIR-AIR
1250-Watt Travel Dryer or

FAIR-AIR
**Curling Iron/Styling
Brush Combo**

only $9

(a savings of $1.97 per appliance)

Progress Check 4

Use the ads to answer each question. Write your answers on a separate piece of paper.

1. Which product is not needed for personal appearance? How much does it cost?
2. If you buy all three Fair-Air appliances at the bonus price, how much will that be? How much would all three appliances cost at the regular price?
3. How much would you save on the Steam-Easy Iron by buying it at the special price?
4. Why do you think there is a limit of two bottles of Creamy Skin lotion per customer?

What Else Will You Have to Buy?

Besides buying for your total appearance, you'll need to buy other personal things. Again, what you buy depends on what you do. You may need things for your job or for school. Or you may need things to use in your spare time.

For example, you may have to buy tools or equipment for your job. At school, you'll need books, notebooks, and pens. For your personal interests, you may need fishing equipment, car magazines, or garden tools. Or you may want art supplies or film for your camera. Again, you have to make choices. Which things must you have? Which things do you want but can do without? What can you afford?

Basics Practice

a. 8 A.M. to noon = how many hours?

b. noon to 11 P.M. = how many hours?

c. 8 A.M. to 11 P.M. = how many hours?

Progress Check 5

Use a separate piece of paper. Write down your three main activities during waking hours. Next to each activity, list the number of hours you spend per day doing these things.

Now write down the number of hours you are normally awake. (For example, if you're up from 7 A.M. to midnight, you'd write 17 hours.)

Next, figure what percentage of your day is spent on each activity. The largest percentages are where your money for new things will probably go.

When Is a Sale a Good Sale?

How do you know if a special-priced item is really a good deal? When you see a price that is lower than usual, you'll want to know how the items compare with items that are not on sale. Ask yourself these questions:

What is the **size** of what you're buying? If you're buying a tent, a rug, or a candy bar, you need to know how big it is. The item might cost less because it is smaller.

Here's a Tip: Don't buy anything on sale that you wouldn't buy at a regular price. A low price isn't a good reason to get something you'll never use.

What is the **quantity**? If you're buying tapes, socks, or flashbulbs, how many are in the package? The item might cost less because there are fewer in the package.

What is the **quality**? If you're buying a watch or a beach towel, how good is it? Is it a brand-name watch? Is it watertight? Will the company replace the watch if it stops working a year, or ten years, from now? Is the towel thick and well-made? Or do you see loose threads or snags? Sometimes low prices mean that the product is cheaply made and won't last very long.

Progress Check 6

Write your answers on a separate piece of paper.

1. You see an ad for a cooler chest for $7.97. Another one is advertised for $17.97. You find out that the $7.97 chest holds seven quarts. The one for $17.97 holds 55 quarts. How much do you pay per quart for every quart that the smaller chest holds? That the larger chest holds? You want the cooler that costs less per quart. Which one will you buy?

2. Batteries are on sale. They're $3.99 for a package of four. What is the cost of each battery in the four-pack? A two-pack battery package costs $2.29. What is the cost of each of the batteries in the two-pack? Compare the cost of the batteries in the four-pack and the two-pack. Which is the better deal—two of the two-pack battery packages or one four-pack package?

What to Watch Out For in Ads

Ads can be tricky. Sometimes they don't give you all the information you need. Sometimes they include the information in very small print or in a different part of the ad. Take a look at this camera ad.

Home Filmer 8mm Sound-Movie Camera with Remote Control and Timer

$997 only $43/Month*

*with a Circus City Charge Card. Subject to credit approval.

It says you can pay $43 a month for the camera. But next to the offer, you see an **asterisk**, or star. This means you're to look at the bottom of the ad. There you'll find a sentence with an asterisk in front of it. It says that you need the store's charge card plus a good credit rating with that store.

When you read an ad, check to see if the price includes any of these extra costs:

- delivering big items to your home.
- putting the parts together (assembly fees).
- hooking up the item to your water or electrical system (installation fees).

Sometimes these extra costs, or fees, add a lot to the total price.

How Store Owners Convince You to Buy

Store owners want you to shop at their stores. They advertise items in a way that will make people want to buy them. One way they do this is to offer items at **wholesale** prices.

The wholesale price is what the store pays for an item. Then a **markup** is added to make the **retail** price. But not always. Take a look at this ad:

Ski Wear <u>below</u> Wholesale
Up to 70% off
SUMMER SALE

Notice that the store is offering to sell ski wear *below* wholesale. If you owned a store, would you sell things for less than you paid for them?

Would you make money if you did? Of course not. Be careful of wholesale bargains. The prices may be low, but they're probably not wholesale.

Progress Check 7

Write your answers on a separate piece of paper.

Suppose you own a T-shirt shop. You pay $1.50 for each shirt. Then you put on lettering that costs you 50¢. You sell the shirts at a marked-up price of $8.75 each. How much money do you make on one shirt? A dozen is twelve. How much do you make on a dozen?

Sometimes a store will run a big ad, saying something like this:

BIGGEST CLOTHING SALE THIS SPRING!

You get to the store on the morning of the sale. The item you want isn't there. A salesperson tells you the item is sold out. The item you wanted was probably very popular. The store used it as bait. The bait got you into the store.

Look for this statement in ads: *All merchandise subject to prior sale.* This means that the item you want may be sold by the time you get there. The store didn't have very many of the items to begin with.

Now read this ad.

WE'RE GIVING AWAY **$2,000**
Worth of Merchandise Certificates
FREE 1ST 200 people Saturday only!
Ten-dollar Certificates to be applied to any purchase over $50.
Limit one ten-dollar merchandise certificate per person, per purchase.
Bills are coded & must be used the same day issued.

"We're giving away $2,000" attracts your attention. But notice that the most you can get is a ten-dollar certificate. And in order to use it, you have to spend at least fifty dollars.

Progress Check 8

Write your answers on a separate piece of paper.

1. Gina is the 189th person in the store on Saturday. She gets a $10 certificate. It's good only on that day, and only if she buys something for more than $50. She buys something for $65. She uses her certificate. How much cash does she pay? What percentage of her total purchase is subtracted from her bill?

2. Louise spends $100 in the store. Her ten-dollar certificate brings her total down to $90. What percentage does she save?

Math on the Job

1. Florinda Gonzales runs a clothing store. She is marking prices down for a sale. She has to be careful not to cut the prices so low that the store can't make money. The coat she is pricing was marked up to $130 from its wholesale price of $70. How much money did Florinda's store make on the coat originally? How much will it make if she marks the price down 40%?

2. Jesse Brickman has to wear a uniform on the job. He is allergic to wool. He has to check the labels of uniforms he buys to make sure the cloth has no wool in it. One uniform is 40% cotton. The rest is wool. What percentage of the uniform is made of wool? Can Jesse wear it?

Chapter Review

Chapter Summary

- Your health, your appearance, and the way you spend your time decide many of your personal purchases.

- It doesn't pay to save money at the expense of your health.

- The clothes you spend the most on should be the ones you'll wear most often.

- Figure out where the largest percentage of your time is spent. Then you'll know what kind of items it makes sense to buy.

- When reading ads, find out what you can about quality, quantity, and size.

- Watch out for tricky ads. Some ads have fine print you need to read. Some ads make promises that aren't entirely true.

Chapter Quiz

Write your answers on a separate sheet of paper.

1. Henry sprains his shoulder playing basketball. He doesn't get it checked. His shoulder gets worse. He stays off work for two days. He loses $76 in pay. Finally he pays $35 for a visit to the doctor. He has to pay $19 for medicine because by now his shoulder is swollen. How much might Henry have saved by visiting the doctor right away?

2. Charlotte is going camping. She needs a sleeping bag at $75, a tent at $159, a lantern at $18.95, cooking utensils at $45, and a new camera at $150. Which things would she buy if she had only enough money for something to sleep in and an emergency light? How much would she spend? How much more would she need to buy all the other things?

3. Darlene wants to buy a small study lamp. She sees one on sale for $7.99. The ad says *all-metal construction, baked enamel finish.* She sees another lamp for $6. It says, *heavy-duty plastic.* How much more would she need to pay for a metal lamp rather than a plastic one?

4. When buying any item, you need to think about:

   a. quality, quantity, size.

   b. wholesale cost, discounts, contracts.

   c. stores, cars, checking.

5. Why don't most stores offer below-wholesale prices?

Challenge

Look at the various advertisements in the paper. Choose one item that you would like to buy. It can be a coat, a volleyball, a video game—or anything at all. Now find as many ads as you can for that one item. Compare what the ads say. How many of them tell about size, color, quantity, quality, or special credit offers? Read each ad very carefully, especially the small print. Then select the store where you'd buy the item. Write a paragraph telling why you selected that store.

12 Getting the Best Buy

Wise buyers compare price and quality before they make a decision.

Chapter Learning Objectives

- Name the best times of year to find bargains on personal items.
- Figure the difference among discount prices, sale prices, and retail prices.
- Name ways to save time and money when buying personal items.
- Define special terms used on catalog order forms.
- Figure tax, shipping, and handling for items bought through a catalog.
- Review basic math skills in the Appendix at the back of this textbook.

Words to Know

catalog   a listing of products you can order and have sent to you

clearance sale   an event in which many items are marked down for quick sale

discount   the amount taken off a regular price

factory outlet   a self-service, low-priced store that sells items directly from the factory where they were made

merchandise   goods for sale; articles bought and sold

minimum   the least possible amount

storewide   throughout the whole store

Getting the Best Bargains on Personal Items

When buying personal items, there are ways to save both dollars and hours. Here are three of those ways:

1. Buy at the "bargain" times of year when shopping at retail stores.
2. Shop at **factory outlets** and **discount** stores.
3. Buy from **catalogs** that offer reduced, or discount, prices.

Which Sales Are the Best?

There are three excellent times of the year to shop at retail stores. During these times, most retail stores hold **storewide clearance sales**.

These sales happen:

- after Christmas.
- after Easter.
- after summer holidays, like the 4th of July.

There are also other times to shop for bargains. It depends on what you want to buy.

Suppose you want to buy shoes. You'd like to buy them on sale. Look at the Sale Calendar. It lists when certain personal items go on sale.

Sale Calendar

January	February	March	April
cosmetics	men's shirts	winter coats	dresses
men's coats	air conditioners		men's suits
dresses	cosmetics		women's coats
men's shirts	curtains		
jewelry			
shoes			
handbags			
linens/blankets			

May	June	July	August
blankets	dresses	men's shirts	school clothes
		swimsuits (after July 4th)	swimsuits
		men's shoes	men's coats
		women's shoes	linens
		handbags	

September	October	November	December
cosmetics	school clothes	dresses	men's suits
		men's suits	women's coats
		women's coats	shoes
		shoes	blankets
		blankets	

Wordwise: A *white sale* is a sale on linens, such as sheets, towels, and tablecloths. The best time for this is January and August.

Find the best month or months to buy shoes. You'll discover that January, July, November, and December are the times that shoes go on sale.

Now think of some other personal item. Do you need a shirt, a swimsuit, a dress, or a coat? Find the best time to buy that item.

Progress Check 1

Use the Sale Calendar to answer these questions. Write your answers on a separate piece of paper.

1. What would be the best time to buy a swimsuit?

2. Which two months are the best for buying school clothes?

3. What would be the best three months for buying men's suits?

4. Suppose you see a sweater you want to buy in December. The sweater is $65.95. In January, it sells for 40% off. How much will you save on the sweater by buying it in January? How much will you pay for the sweater in January?

Basics Practice

a. $42.90 x .30 = ?

b. $42.95
        − 12.89

c. $145.00 x .25 = ?

Calculator Practice

Step 1:

Enter 65.95

Press x

Enter .40

Press =

Your discount should be: $26.38

(continued on next page)

Step 2:

Enter 65.95

Press −

Enter discount

Press =

The January price should be: $39.57

---

5. On June 27, you see a pair of shoes you've been looking for. They're $47. You wait until the sale after the 4th of July. The shoes are marked down to $32. How much did you save by waiting a couple of weeks?

6. You and your brother buy a watch for your mother's Christmas present. It costs $165. During the second week of January, all watches are 35% off. How much more did you pay in December than you would have paid in January?

Why Buy by the Bunch?

Sometimes you can save 10% to 30% by buying things in quantity. Items such as undershirts, shorts, handkerchiefs, and pantyhose may be priced by the twos or threes. Or they may be sold in packages. For example, socks that sell at $3.50 a pair might be sold at two pairs for $6. You would save $1 by buying two pairs.

Solve It

1. One undershirt sells for $4.50. A package of three of the same undershirts sells for $11.25. How much does each shirt in the package cost? ($11.25 ÷ 3 = ?)

2. How much would you save on each shirt by buying the package deal? ($4.50 – price of each shirt in the package = ?)

How Do Discount Stores and Factory Outlets Work?

Sometimes a factory makes too many of one item. The extra items might then be sold at a discount store or factory outlet.

Sometimes items aren't perfect, but you can't tell by looking at them. Then they're marked *irregular* or *flawed*. These also might be sold at a discount store or factory outlet.

A factory outlet can offer big savings. An outlet that carries designer labels can sell things for as much as 50% off.

Vannessa tried on a high-fashion coat that fit her perfectly. She wanted to buy it but the retail price was $275. She couldn't afford it. A month later, she went to the designer's discount outlet. She saw the same coat at 50% off. What will she save if she buys the coat at the outlet? To find the answer, multiply the retail price by .50 (for 50%).

Calculator Practice

Coat Savings

Enter 275

Press x

Enter .50

Press =

Vanessa will save $137.50 on the coat

Progress Check 2

1. The jeans you like cost $37 retail. The same jeans cost 25% less at a discount store. How much is the discount? ($37 x .25 = ?) How much do the jeans cost at the discount store? (Subtract the 25% discount from the retail price.)

2. The collar size isn't perfect on some shirts made to sell for $52 each. The shirts are marked *irregular.* They are marked down 30%. How much is taken off the $52 price? How much will one irregular shirt cost?

3. Slacks made to fit numbered sizes cost $42. Similar slacks marked *small, medium,* and *large* cost 10% less. How much do the small, medium, and large slacks cost?

What's a List Price?

Sometimes you'll see ads that say things like this.

RECORDS AND TAPES, MANUFACTURER'S LIST PRICE $12.99, OUR PRICE $7.99

The *list price* is the retail price suggested by the company that made the item. Most items don't normally sell at list price. When you see *list price,* use the price of the item in another store for comparison. If the price is really less, then you have a good deal.

Saving Time Shopping

There are ways to save your time as well as your money.

• Call various stores and ask for what you want. Compare their prices before you visit the stores.

• Shop by using a catalog.

Here's a Tip: Not all catalogs offer bargains, but many do. You need to compare their prices to those at the stores near you.

Calling first saves time and carfare. And it helps you locate the best price.

By shopping from catalogs, you cut out carfare costs entirely. You also save time and parking fees. Many catalogs have prices lower than those at the stores where you regularly shop. Suppose you see this ad in a catalog:

$30 OFF WALK 'N LISTEN STEREO HEADPHONES, AUTO REVERSE CASSETTE. USES *AA* BATTERIES.

Regularly $129   Now $99

You check prices at local stores, and this is what you find out: The Walk 'n Listen sells at Murray's for $136. It sells at Tracy's for $132.95. You would save a lot by ordering it from the catalog. The savings would more than cover the cost for shipping, or mailing, the item to you.

Solve It

1. What's the difference between Tracy's price and the catalog price?
2. Add a $7.50 shipping charge to the catalog price. That's the amount you might actually pay to buy the Walk 'n Listen from the catalog. How much would it cost you?

Sometimes catalogs list special discounts for buying more than one of an item. For example, if you buy two or more T-shirts, the catalog price is $6.99 each. One T-shirt alone costs $7.49.

Solve It

```
  $7.49   price of one T-shirt
- 6.99   price for each, if two or more ordered
    ?    amount saved per shirt
```

Progress Check 3

Write your answers on a separate sheet of paper.

1. The regular price for a sweatshirt is $12. The catalog discount price for one sweatshirt is $10.49. The discount price for more than one is $9.99 each. How much will you save if you buy one sweatshirt from the catalog?

2. How much will you save on each sweatshirt if you buy two of them from the catalog?

Placing an Order from a Catalog

You can order almost anything from a catalog—clothes, sports equipment, luggage, telephones, jewelry, and books. Catalogs have order forms that you fill out for the items you want to buy. Then you send the form to the company along with your check, money order, or credit card number.

All order blanks do not look exactly the same, but they are similar. Most order blanks ask you to write:

a. the name of the item.
b. the number the item has in the catalog.
c. the color you want.
d. the size you need.
e. how many of the item you want.
f. the price of each item.

The order blank will also ask you to figure:

a. the total price of the item (the price x how many of that item).
b. the total price of all the items you order.
c. the shipping charge (how much it will cost to send the items to your home).

d. the handling charge (the cost of preparing and packing the item).
e. the sales tax (if any).
f. the total price of the order (b through e, added together).

Sometimes you will see abbreviations. *Qty.* means quantity. *Ship. wt.* means the shipping weight of the item you're buying. If you're asked to give the shipping weight, it's listed where your item is described.

Suppose you want to order these things: a watch, a skirt, and a pair of men's pants. Read what the catalog says about each item.

The watch:

Geometrical dial and expandable band. Quartz movement. From Seville. Warranted.

(1 lb)	Z	13	125	049	Silver	
	Z	13	125	050	Gold	$35.00

The skirt:

Full skirt, pleated front; soft, matching fabric belt; cotton knit. Machine wash.

Sizes 4, 6, 8, 10, 12, 14, 16

	C	23	192	1602	Blue	
	C	23	192	1603	Green	
(2 lbs. 13 oz.)						$39.00

The pants:

Shoreman's jeans. 100% cotton pants, front and back pockets, straight legs.

	A	22	192	1639	Gray	
	A	22	192	1640	Tan	

Sizes 29–40
(2 lbs. 6 oz.) $32.00

Progress Check 4

Write your answers on a separate piece of paper.

Imagine you are going to buy the watch, skirt, and pants. The delivery charge for them is $9.25, the handling charge is $1.50, and the total tax is $8.93.

1. How much will you pay for all these items (including charges and tax)?
2. You decide you don't want the watch. Your handling price will stay the same. Your delivery charge is $1.50 less. Your tax is $1.43 less. How much will your total cost be now?
3. Make an order form to use for buying the shirt or pants from the catalog. Label spaces for writing in:
    a. the name of the item.
    b. its catalog number.
    c. the size you want.
    d. its weight.
    e. its price.
    f. the quantity, or number, you wish to order.

Then fill in your order form. Be sure to use the catalog number shown for the color you want.

Figuring Out Shipping and Handling

Usually when you order from a catalog, you need to figure out shipping and handling charges. These are the two amounts the company charges for packaging and sending the **merchandise** to you. Sometimes it'll be a flat amount. This means one price no matter what or how much your order. Other times shipping and handling is figured by how much you buy.

Look at the shipping and handling chart on the facing page. Notice that it says "**minimum** merchandise order $5.00" at the bottom. This means $5.00 worth of merchandise is the smallest amount you can buy.

PLEASE NOTE

Avoid delay. Be sure to include shipping and handling. Simply add the cost from this easy-to-figure chart to the total amount of your order.

PLEASE ADD FOR SHIPPING & HANDLING

Up to $6.00	Add $1.95
$6.01 to $8.00	Add $2.25
$8.01 to $10.00	Add $2.75
$10.01 to $15.00	Add $3.25
$15.01 to $20.00	Add $3.75
$20.01 to $30.00	Add $4.45
Over $30.00	Add $4.95

Packages sent to separate addresses require separate postage.

MINIMUM MERCHANDISE ORDER $5.00

Progress Check 5

Basics Practice

a. $8.39
    + 2.52

b. $7.33
     15.00
    + 3.29

c. $11.20
    x .40

Write your answers on a separate piece of paper.

1. What is the minimum merchandise order at this company? What if you wanted to order something that was $3.29? How much more would you need to spend to send in an order?

2. What would you pay for shipping and handling if you ordered $7.62 worth of merchandise?

3. You place an order for these items: socks for $8.98, a game for $7.49, and a poster for $13.00. How much shipping and handling will you pay?

On the next page is another type of shipping and handling chart. When you use this one, you will figure what you owe by using percentages. For 10%, multiply by .10. For 6%, multiply by .06. For 5%, multiply by .05.

Shipping and Handling

$2.00 – $25.00 ....Add $2.50
$25.00 – $50.00 ....Add 10%
$50.00 – $100.00 ....Add 6%
$100.00+ ....Add 5%

Calculator Practice

 Suppose you ordered $32 worth of clothes. How much would you add for shipping and handling?

Enter 32

Press x

Enter .10

Press =

Your shipping and handling costs are: $3.20

Suppose you ordered $54.75 worth of books and tapes. How much would you add for shipping and handling?

Enter 54.75

Press x

Enter .06

Press =

Your shipping and handling costs are: $.33

The order form will have a subtotal that is the cost of the items you've bought. You add the shipping and handling to this subtotal. Sometimes you'll also need to add tax.

Look at the bottom of this delivery form. The subtotal is filled in for you. There are spaces for the cost of sales tax and shipping and handling. There's also a space for the total amount you must pay.

subtotal:	$44.50
sales tax:	_____
shipping and handling:	_____
TOTAL ENCLOSED:	_____

Progress Check 6

Write your answers on a separate piece of paper.

1. Imagine there's a sales tax of 6%. Figure the amount of sales tax on the items in this order.

2. Suppose the shipping and handling rate for $44.50 is 8%. What would that amount be?

3. What would be the total charge for tax, and shipping and handling? How much money should you enclose?

Math on the Job

1. Elvin Harris manages a clothing store. He decides to put the $32.50 jeans on sale for 20% below the retail price. How much does Elvin cut off the price? What is the new sale price for the jeans?

2. Myra Watson's catalog company sells the same jeans for $23 plus 10% for shipping and handling. Would ordering the jeans through Myra's catalog cost less than the jeans on sale at Elvin's store? What would be the difference in cost to you?

Chapter Review

Chapter Summary

- The best times of the year to buy personal items on sale are after Christmas, after Easter, and after holidays like the 4th of July.

- Sometimes buying in quantity can save you money. You can buy things in pairs or packages.

- Discount stores offer reduced prices on many things you need.

- Factory outlets can offer savings as high as 50%.

- It's a good idea to check prices at different stores to see how they compare. Then you'll know if an item has been greatly reduced from its regular, retail price.

- You can often save time and money by doing two things: you can call stores and compare prices before you shop, and you can order from catalogs.

- When you place an order for items in a catalog, you need to fill out a form.

- On an order form, you'll often fill in various amounts. These may include shipping and handling charges and sales tax. You'll always need to figure the total amount you must pay.

Chapter Quiz

Write your answers on a separate sheet of paper.

1. Name the three best times of the year to shop at storewide sales.

2. Andrew sees a suit he'd like to buy in December. It's $155. In January it's advertised at a 40% discount. How much will it cost in January?

3. Dominick wants to buy three pairs of sport socks. They're advertised at $2.95 a pair at one store, two pairs for $5.00 at another store, and three pairs for $6.75 at a third store. Which is the least expensive way to buy them?

4. At a discount store, Cathy sees a leather jacket that is marked *flawed*. She doesn't see anything wrong with it, and it's marked 40% off the retail price of $295. What is the discounted price of the jacket?

5. Rosa is purchasing $64.79 worth of camping gear from a catalog. She needs to add the sales tax. The tax in her state is 6%. Find the amount of tax Rosa should write on the order form.

6. Valerie is purchasing items from a catalog. Their subtotal is $33.36. The tax is $2.00. The shipping and handling charge is $4.95. What amount should be on Valerie's check or money order?

7. What is meant by *shipping charges*? What is meant by *handling charges*?

Challenge

Write your own description of a watch that you will sell in a catalog. Try to make the reader want to buy the watch. Advertise that your watch will sell for 40% off the regular price. Then figure out what the watch's regular price will be. Figure out what the sale price will be.

Unit Six Review

Answer the questions below. Look back at Chapters 11 and 12 if you need help.

1. List three important things to consider when planning personal spending.

2. Give an example of why it could cost a lot to put off regular check-ups at the dentist.

3. What kinds of clothes might you need if you worked as a forest ranger in snowy Alaska? What if, instead, you worked as a pizza cook in sunny Florida? Would your clothing needs differ? If so, how and why?

4. Why is it important to look at the small print at the bottom of an ad?

5. Explain why a new watch priced at $10 might not be a very good deal.

6. Explain why some people wait to buy swimsuits in July or August or school clothes in October.

7. Which place would probably have the highest price on a wool suit—a retail department store, a factory outlet, or a discount store? Why?

8. Name one way you could save time *and* money on gifts for the December holidays.

9. You are filling out an order form in a catalog. You fill in the subtotal. Then you write the total amount enclosed for your purchases. Why might the total be a higher amount than the subtotal?

10. A catalog form says: *MINIMUM MERCHANDISE ORDER $10*. What does this mean?

Unit Seven

Owning a Vehicle

13 Buying a Vehicle

A car is a big investment. Careful shopping will help you get the most for your money.

Chapter Learning Objectives

- Make a list of things to think about when buying a car.
- Interpret Blue Book listings of car prices.
- Compare dealer prices to Blue Book prices.
- Use a loan table and figure monthly payments.
- Figure the amount of a down payment.
- Review basic math skills in the Appendix at the end of this textbook.

Words to Know

annual percentage rate   the amount (in percent) of the finance charge

balance of the loan   the amount left to pay

Blue Book   a book that shows the wholesale and retail prices of cars

car insurance   protection you buy against the cost of car accidents and theft

dealer   a business person who sells cars or other items

finance charge   a fee for borrowing money

loan   money that is borrowed

mileage   the total miles a car has been driven; also the average number of miles a car will go on a gallon of gas

Thinking About Transportation

You have a good job. You also have a place to live and some things of your own. But if you're like most working people, you have to travel to get to work. So you need to make another decision. What are your transportation needs?

Is your job close to home? Could you walk to work or ride a bicycle? This would keep your transportation costs very low. Perhaps you could even find a good deal on a used bicycle.

Could you share rides with people at work? Or is your job near a public transportation route? Usually bus or subway fares are reasonable. And regular riders can often save money by buying monthly fare books or passes.

But suppose walking, bicycling, or public transportation is not the answer for you. You decide that you need your own car. If so, it's time to think about what kind of car makes sense for you.

Car Dreams, Car Choices

Did You Know?
In one year, Americans drive their cars more than 1 trillion miles. If you made 5,000 trips between Earth and the sun, you wouldn't go that far!

You may say, "Oh, I'd look great sitting behind the wheel of a brand new convertible!" You may say, "I'd really like to drive around in a bright red sports car!"

Most people think this way when they first decide to buy a car. It's fun to imagine the car you want most. But it doesn't help you figure out the car you need.

The car you need is the one that matches up with the way you live and how much you earn.

Making the Big Decision

Some cars are safer than others. They cost less to insure. Some are expensive or difficult to fix. Some use a lot of gas. The cost of **car insurance**, gas, and repairs can really add up when you own certain kinds of cars.

Here are some other things to think about when you get ready to buy a car.

Wordwise: A stick shift is also called a *standard,* or *manual, transmission.*

1. Can you drive a car that has a stick shift, or do you need an automatic?
2. Will you usually need your car for long trips or for short ones?
3. How many people will be riding in your car?
4. Will you need to carry heavy loads or equipment?

5. What type of climate will your car be in?

6. Will your car be parked outside or inside most of the time?

Think about your answers to the questions. What do they tell you about the car you need? Maybe your car is going to make lots of long trips. Then it must not be too old. It should be in very good condition.

Maybe you'll be driving alone most of the time. If so, then a 2-door car will do. If you'll have passengers, you may need a 4-door car.

If you carry heavy loads or equipment, you'll need a heavier car. It will need to have lots of trunk space. You might even consider a pickup truck.

Will your car be parked outside most of the time? Then you won't want a brightly colored car. Bright colors can fade in the sun.

If you'll be using your car in a very hot climate, you may want an air conditioner. If you live in a rainy climate, you won't need a sunroof.

What Kind of Car Is the Best Buy?

You can get books at the library that will tell you about the best cars to buy. These books explain how well certain cars drive. They tell which cars have the best motors, and how much gas the cars use.

Study them to see which cars, new or used, sound right for you. Write down the names of those cars.

Using a Blue Book

The **Blue Book** is a useful guide book. You can look at it in the library.

The Blue Book gives you the price that the car probably cost the **dealer**. This wholesale price is called *low book*. The Blue Book also gives you the usual retail price of the car. This is called *high book*. The retail price is the price the customer pays.

They're Not All the Same: Cars come in many different body styles. In a Blue Book, 2D means two-door. What do you think 4D means?

The Blue Book is especially helpful when you want to buy a used car. A Blue Book page will list the year and name of the car. It will also give the name of the model and tell its model number, weight, and original price (the list price). You will also find two very important items of information on the page. Look at the listing for the 1983 Chevrolet. These two items are circled for you. Here is what they mean:

Whls. means *wholesale* price or *low book*.

Sug. Ret. means *suggested retail* or *high book*.

1983 CHEVROLET

Body Type	VIN	Wt.	List	Whls.	Sug. Ret.

CHEVROLET
1982 CHEVROLET - Use Older Car Guide. See p. 2
1983 CHEVROLET - 1G1A(J08C)-D-#
Chevette — 4-Cyl. — Equipment Schedule D
W.B. 94.3', 97.3" (4D); CID 98.

Body Type	VIN	Wt.	List	Whls.	Sug. Ret.
Scooter Hatchback 2D	J08C	1971	5765	**1000**	**1900**
Scooter Hatchback 4D	J68C	2040	6101	**1075**	**2000**
Hatchback Coupe 2D	B08C	2029	6033	**1175**	**2125**
Hatchback Sedan 4D	B68C	2090	6180	**1250**	**2225**
4-Cyl. Diesel Engine	D	—	—	**(475)**	**(635)**

You can use the Blue Book listing to figure out what you should pay for your car. Find the suggested retail price of the car. It's listed on the right. If the car you want costs more than this high-book price, it might not be a very good deal.

Progress Check 1

Use the Blue Book listing to answer these questions. Write your answers on a separate piece of paper.

Here's a Tip: Most used cars should be priced between the wholesale and retail price in the Blue Book. They should not be above retail unless they are very special.

1. What is the wholesale price of a 1983 Chevette Scooter Hatchback 2D?
2. What is the retail price of the same car?
3. Is there much difference between the wholesale and retail price of the 1983 Scooter Hatchback 4D? What is that difference?
4. Which costs more—the 2-door or the 4-door? How much more?
5. Andrea has found the car she wants. The low book on the car is $3,200. The high book is $4,400. Would Andrea expect to pay $4,600 for this car? Why or why not?
6. William is looking at a car with a wholesale price of $3,500. The retail price is $4,900. The dealer is asking $4,795. Does this car look like it might be a good deal? Why or why not?
7. You are buying a $3,500 car in a state that has a 7% sales tax. How much will the tax be?

Shopping for a Car

You have studied different cars. You have compared Blue Book prices to dealers' prices. You know what the reasonable prices are. Now it's time to take a closer look at the cars themselves. You want to shop for the car that meets your needs. You want to find one you can afford to buy.

There are many ways to shop for a car. One way is to look in the classified section of the newspaper. Another is to buy from a used-car lot.

Many people think that it is best to go to a new-car dealer who also sells used cars. This is because the new-car dealer keeps the cars that people trade in when they buy a new car. He or she will sell only the best of these used cars on the used-car lot.

Tips for Finding Reliable Car Dealers

- Ask your friends, relatives, co-workers, or employer to recommend a dealer who can be trusted.
- Go to a dealer who is a member of the National Automobile Association.
- Stay away from a dealer who tries to hurry you. Don't do business with a dealer who does not want to answer your questions.

When you find the car you think might be right for you, do these things:

1. Compare the price of the car to the retail price in the Blue Book.
2. Compare other dealers' prices for the same type of car. Make sure the **mileage** is about the same.
3. Drive the car on the same kinds of roads you will be using.
4. Take the car to a mechanic and have it checked.

Progress Check 2

Suppose you are interested in buying a 1983 two-door Chevette Hatchback coupe. You see it at three different dealers. Here are your choices:

Dealer A	Dealer B	Dealer C
$2,225	$1,500	$1,999

Here's a Tip: You can make an *offer* on a car you like. Check the Blue Book price. Then make an offer that is somewhere between the low-book and high-book price.

Write your answers on a separate piece of paper.

1. Which dealer has the highest price? How much higher is this price than the price of Dealer B?

2. You have looked in the Blue Book. You know that the low book on this car is $1,175. The high book is $2,125. Which dealer's car is priced higher than high book? How much higher?

3. Which dealer comes closest to the low-book price?

Paying for the Car

You have found a good buy on a car. But how will you pay for it? Here are some choices:

- Use your savings and pay cash for the car.
- Take out a car **loan**, make a down payment, and pay off the rest in monthly payments.

How Much Should a Down Payment Be?

Wordwise: An older car is sometimes given to the dealer in place of a down payment on a newer car. This is called a *trade-in*.

A down payment is an amount of cash you pay the dealer first before you start making monthly payments. The down payment is subtracted from the money you owe for the car. The larger your down payment, the smaller your monthly payments will be.

Often a down payment is one-fourth or one-third of the car's price. To find the amount of a down payment that is one-fourth, divide the price of the car by 4. To find the amount of a down payment that is one-third, divide the price of the car by 3.

a. Price of car: $4,385.
   Down payment of $\frac{1}{4}$.
   What is the down payment? $4\overline{)4,385.00}$

b. Price of car: $3,696.
   Down payment of $\frac{1}{3}$.
   What is the down payment? $3\overline{)3,696.00}$

Progress Check 3

Write your answers on a separate piece of paper.

1. The car you want to buy is $1,500. What amount will your down payment be if you pay one-fourth of the price?
2. What amount will your down payment be if you pay one-third of the price?
3. If you pay $500 down on a car that is priced at $1,500, how much will you still owe on the car?

Basics Practice

a. $6,496 \div 4$

b. $3,786$
       $-\ \ 841$

c.   10% of 1,691 =

How Do You Pay Off the Loan?

You make a down payment of $600 on the $1,600 car. Now you need to get a loan for the amount you still owe: $1,000. This is the **balance of the loan**, or the amount that you will pay off in monthly payments.

The Finance Charge chart shows you the different payments you would have to pay monthly on a loan of $1,000.

Finance Charge for a $1000 Loan

	Rate	Number of Months to Pay Back Loan		
		12 months	24 months	36 months
	10%	87.92	46.15	32.27
	11%	88.39	46.61	32.74
	12%	88.85	47.08	33.22
Annual	14%	89.79	48.02	34.18
Percentage	16%	90.74	48.97	35.16
Rates	18%	91.68	49.93	36.16
	20%	92.64	50.90	37.17
	22%	93.60	51.88	38.20
	24%	94.56	52.88	39.24

The **finance charge** is a percentage of the amount of money you are borrowing. This is the money you pay the bank or finance company for making you the loan. Some loans are for 10%. Some are for 12%, and so on. The **Annual Percentage Rate** is shown on the left side of the chart.

Some loans are for 12 months. Some are to be paid back in 24 months or 36 months. The length of the loan is shown at the top of the Finance Charge chart.

Suppose you have a $1,000 loan with a finance charge of 12%. If you took out a two-year loan, how much would you pay each month? To learn the answer, first find the row that lists the 12% rates. Move across the row to the column that shows the 24-month amounts (24 months = 2 years). The amount shown is $47.08. This means you would pay $47.08 each month for 24 months.

Calculator Practice

 Use your calculator to find out how much you would pay altogether on a 36-month loan for $1000 at 16%. First find the monthly payment on the chart.

Enter 35.16

Press x

Enter 36

Press =

You would pay $1,265.76 altogether. What's the difference between this and the $1000 borrowed?

Enter total amount paid altogether.

Press –

Enter 1000

Press =

Your total finance charge (or interest) is: $265.76

Progress Check 4

Here's a Tip: You can get a loan chart at any library. It will show you how much monthly payments will be for many different kinds of loans.

Look at the Finance Charge chart again. Write your answers on a separate piece of paper.

1. Margo borrowed $1,000 for 12 months. What would her monthly payment be if she were going to pay the loan at a finance rate of 16%?

2. George will repay a $1,000 loan in 24 months. The finance charge on the loan is 12%. What will George's monthly payment be?

3. Ray can afford $100 for a monthly car payment. Could he make a monthly payment for 24 months at 12%?

4. Could Ray make a monthly payment for 12 months at 16%? How much would he have left over from his $100?

Where Do You Go for a Loan?

If you decide to take out a loan, you need to find the place that will give you the best deal. You want to pay the *lowest* percentage rate over the shortest period of time. The dealer may offer to finance the car. But you may be able to save money if you get a loan from a bank, a credit union, or the American Automobile Association.

It pays to shop for loans. Compare the finance charges. Also, look over the loan contract carefully. Find out what might happen if you miss a payment.

How Do You Check the Contract?

If there is anything in your contract that you do not understand, make sure you ask the banker or car dealer. By law, they must answer any questions you have about the contract. If you still have any doubts, ask your city's legal aid office for help. You can find their number in the phone book.

Once your first questions are answered, ask yourself these questions too:

1. Are all the blanks in the contract filled in?
2. Does the contract match what the loan officer told me?
3. Does the contract include the amount of my down payment?
4. Has the down payment been subtracted from the price of the car?

If the answer to any of these questions is no, talk to your banker or dealer again. Make sure everything checks out. Then, you can feel confident about signing the contract.

Progress Check 5

Read each paragraph below. Then write your answers on a separate piece of paper.

1. Bill is buying a car for $3,450. He pays $500 in cash as a down payment. The dealer also accepts Bill's old car for another $750 toward the down payment. The dealer offers Bill a two-year car loan for the rest of the money owed. Bill reads the loan contract. It is written up for $2,950. Bill sees that the dealer has made a mistake. What is the mistake? What should the amount of the loan really be?

Calculator Practice

Use your calculator to solve the problem.

Enter 3450

Press –

Enter 500

Press –

Press 750

Press =

Bill owes $2,200 for the car.

2. Vonda applies for a 12-month car loan for $1,000 at 18% interest. She expects to pay $91.68 each month. When she reads the contract, it says: "Payments of $91.68 will be due on the 15th of each month starting February, 1990, and ending February, 1992." Should Vonda sign this loan contract? Why or why not?

Math on the Job

1. Gerald Fitzpatrick is a car dealer. He knows that a fair cost for a car is more than the low-book price but less than the high-book price. He has a car he wants to sell. His wholesale price was $1,375. The suggested retail price is $3,000. What is the difference between the two? If he decides to charge half-way between the two prices, how much will the car cost?

2. Ruthann Johnson has just made her first car sale. The customer is making a $1,250 down payment on a $4,300 car. Ruthann is helping the customer fill out a loan application for the balance. How much does the customer need to borrow to pay for the rest of the cost of the car?

3. Calvin Thomas is a loan officer at a bank. A customer needs to borrow $2,500. The interest rate is 16%. The customer wants to know how much interest he will pay in one year. What should Calvin tell him?

4. Elaine Sanchez owns a car lot. This week she sold five cars at the following prices: $4,898; $2,750; $8,435; and $1,949. What were her total sales for the week?

5. Flossie Gerber works in the office at a used-car lot. Part of her job is to order supplies for the car-washing crew. There are five people in the crew, and they all need new uniforms. Uniforms cost $32.50 each. How much will Flossie have to pay for five new uniforms?

Chapter Review

Chapter Summary

- The right car for you matches the way you live and how much you earn.

- The library has guide books that tell about the best car buys. You can find out how much you should spend on any used car by looking in a Blue Book.

- You can become a wise buyer by comparing dealer prices of any car with its Blue Book price.

- If you don't pay cash for a car, you need to make a down payment and take out a loan for the balance.

- A down payment is the money you must pay up front for a car.

- A finance charge is added to the amount of your car loan.

- A monthly payment must not be more than you can afford.

- A good loan gives you the lowest percentage rate over the shortest period of time.

- When shopping for a loan, you will usually find the best deal at a bank, a credit union, or the American Automobile Association.

- Loans should be compared to see which one has the best terms.

- Contracts should always be read before they are signed.

Chapter Quiz

Read the paragraph. Then fill in the checklist below the paragraph. Copy the numbers and answers on a separate piece of paper.

You are going to buy a car that costs $2,700. The sales tax is $162. You are going to put down half of your savings. Half is $662. The monthly payment on your car loan is $96.03 for 24 months.

1. The price of my car, including taxes _____
2. The down payment I am going to make _____
3. The amount I need to borrow _____
4. The amount of each monthly payment _____
5. The number of monthly payments _____
6. The total amount of monthly payments _____
7. The cost of the interest on the car loan _____

Challenge

Which sounds like the easiest and least expensive way to buy a car? Why?

1. Make no down payment. Pay on a 12% loan for 18 months.
2. Trade in a car. Make an additional down payment of $500 and pay off a loan.
3. Save enough money for the car. Then pay cash for it.
4. Pay on a 16% loan for 24 months.
5. Buy a new car and pay for it for 3 years.

14 Maintaining a Vehicle

Car insurance is required by law. A good insurance agent will help you get the most coverage for the least money.

Chapter Learning Objectives

- Answer questions often asked by an insurance agent.
- Compare insurance rates among different companies and places to live.
- Figure collision and comprehensive costs after the deductible is paid.
- Figure a car's mileage per month.
- Interpret a car repair bill.
- Review basic math skills in the Appendix at the back of this book.

Words to Know

collision   insurance that pays for the repair of your car after an accident

comprehensive   insurance that covers damage from such things as fire and flood

coverage   protection against the costs of accidents, theft, or other risks

deductible   the amount of money you pay for repairs or injuries before the insurance company pays

liability   insurance that pays for other people's injuries and property damage if you caused the accident

maximum   the greatest possible amount

premium   money paid to a company for insurance

uninsured motorist coverage   insurance that pays for some of your costs if an uninsured driver hits your car

warranty   a promise that something a company sells will last a certain time, or else you will get money back

After I Buy My Car—Then What?

After you buy your car, you may want to drive it right away. But before you do, you must insure your car. Car insurance protects you in case of an accident. It also protects your car when you are not in it.

You will probably want to have these types of **coverage**: **liability**, medical payments, **uninsured motorist**, **collision**, and **comprehensive**.

Here's a Tip: If you work for a big company or belong to a union, you may be able to get low-cost group insurance.

It pays to shop for good insurance. You want to get the best insurance at the lowest price.

You will need to compare the rates, or prices, insurance companies charge. Begin this way. Ask three people you trust to tell you the name of a good insurance company. Write down the names of the companies. Then call each company. Talk to an agent who sells the insurance. Find out the rate each company will charge you for the same kind of insurance.

The insurance agent will ask you some questions. The agent needs to know some things about you. Then he or she can tell you the insurance rate.

What Does the Insurance Agent Need to Know?

Many things can make a difference in the insurance rate, or **premium**, you pay. To find out what this rate will be, the agent may ask you questions like these:

1. Are you insured now?
2. How old are you?
3. Have you had a good driving record for the past five years?
4. What kind of car do you drive?
5. How far do you drive to work or school?
6. Are you single or married?
7. Where do you live?

Some of these things are the facts now. Some of them may change later. For example, your age will change and you may move to a new job or town.

Progress Check 1

Imagine you're talking to an insurance agent. On a separate piece of paper, write your answers to all seven questions listed on page 224.

Figuring Your Coverage and Rates

Your insurance agent will offer you many choices. You need to talk about different kinds of risks. You also have to think about how much money you want the insurance company to pay in case of theft, fire, or damage. This is called coverage. The more coverage you have, the higher your yearly rates will be. But more coverage also gives you more protection if you have a big accident.

The region, or place where you live, may also make a big difference in your insurance rate. Different places have different rates. Do you live in the country? Then your rate will be much lower than if you live in the city.

Liability Coverage

15/30/5

Region	Basic Rate
A	$115
B	100
C	90
D	110

The chart at the left shows you the basic yearly rates for liability coverage that is 15/30/5. This means that if you have this coverage, the insurance company will pay $15,000 for each person injured in an accident. It will pay $30,000 **maximum** for all persons injured. And it will pay $5,000 maximum for damage to another person's property.

Rates vary by region, or place. Four different regions are listed on the left. The basic rates are on the right.

Progress Check 2

Did You Know?
In most states, it is against the law to drive without liability insurance.

Write your answers on a separate piece of paper.

1. How much higher is the rate in Region A than the rate in Region D?
2. How much higher is the rate in Region A than the rate in Region C?

Your age, your driving record, and the number of miles you drive will also affect how much you pay.

There is another thing that will make a difference in your rate. It is something you can decide for yourself. It is the amount of your **deductible**. This is the amount you must pay to fix your car after an accident. You would pay the deductible first. Then the insurance company would pay the rest. For example, your deductible may be $200 if you're in an accident. This is the deductible on your collision coverage. If your car is damaged by a storm, fire, or other natural event, your deductible may be $100. This is the deductible on your comprehensive coverage. If you agree to a higher deductible, your insurance cost will be lower.

Progress Check 3

Write your answers on a separate piece of paper.

1. Glenda has a collision deductible of $200. A man backing out of his driveway hits the door of her car. He smashes it in. He has no insurance of his own. Glenda is lucky because she is not hurt. But the cost to fix the door is $327.38. How much of this will Glenda pay? How much will the insurance company pay?

2. Sally has a comprehensive deductible of $100. Her car is parked outside in a big storm. The wind is so strong it knocks down a tree. A branch from the tree hits her car and dents the roof. Repairs will cost $682.53. How much will Sally pay? How much will her insurance company pay?

3. Ricky has a collision deductible of $200. He is driving too fast. He turns a corner. His car slides up against a metal mailbox at the curb. The mailbox scratches his car from the hood to the rear fender. Ricky wants to get his car painted. It will cost $837.39. How much will Ricky pay? How much will the insurance company pay?

Discounts for Low-mileage Drivers

You may pay less on your insurance if you drive your car less than a certain number of miles a year.

Do you know how to estimate the number of miles you drive a year? Keep track of how many miles you go in one month. These are counted by the meter on your car called an *odometer*. Let's say your odometer reads 35,423 on May 1. On June 1, it reads 35,729. How many miles did you travel in one month?

Solve It

You would find out by figuring the difference between the two like this:

$$
\begin{array}{rl}
35{,}729 & \text{miles on June 1} \\
-\,35{,}423 & \text{miles on May 1} \\
\hline
306 & \text{number of miles driven} \\
& \text{between May 1 and June 1}
\end{array}
$$

Progress Check 4

Write your answers on a separate piece of paper.

1. The odometer on Florence's car shows 47,211 miles on December 12. On January 12, the odometer shows 47,992. How many miles did Florence travel in a month?
2. If Debra travels 460 miles a month, how many miles will she travel in a year? (A year is 12 months.)

Calculator Practice

Hector's insurance company gives a discount for driving less than 7,500 miles a year. Can Hector get a discount if he travels 312 miles a month?

Enter 312

Press x

Then enter 12 (number of months in a year)

Press = Hector travels 3,744 miles a year.

Is this number more or less than 7,500? Can Hector get a discount?

How Do You Keep Your Car from Breaking Down?

Would you expect to go day after day with no food and water? Of course not! So remember to check your car's food and water, too. Your car won't go without gas. It won't run very long without oil or water, either. When you stop for gas, check the oil and water. Add oil if your car is a quart or more low. Also add water, if needed.

a.
```
    12,832
 -   6,131
```

b.
```
     1,021
 x      12
```

c.
```
    472.95
    111.42
 +   16.18
```

You should take your car in for a check-up and oil change at least every 7,500 miles. When you change your oil, write down how many miles you have on your odometer. Then you know when to change it again.

Progress Check 5

Write your answers on a separate piece of paper.

1. The last time you changed the oil in your car, the odometer read 10,620. Now it reads 15,999. How many miles have you driven since the last change? How many more miles can your car go before it needs a 7,500-mile oil change?

2. The last time you had your oil changed, your odometer read 22,220. Now it reads 29,220. How many more miles can you drive until your car needs an oil change?

What Kind of Tires Should You Buy?

Sooner or later, your car will need tires. It pays to shop for good ones. You will see all kinds of ads for tires. There are several things to think about when you choose a tire.

Here are some facts about tires. These facts may help you know what you want to buy.

Kind of tire:	How long it will last:
Radial	about 40,000 miles
Belted bias	about 25,000 miles
Bias ply	about 15,000–20,000 miles

Check the **warranty** when you are choosing tires. A warranty is a promise made by the tire company. The company promises that the tire will last for a certain number of miles. A 40,000-mile warranty is better than a 25,000-mile warranty.

If the tire does not last the number of promised miles, you get a new tire free. If you have a limited warranty, you will get money off the price of a new tire. The amount depends on how many miles you have gone on the old tire.

Look at the ad below. Read the information next to both tires.

RIDGEWAY TIRES

Firebreak is proud to announce the addition of the Ridgeway tire line to our other great product lines.

Ridgeway Domestic

Steel Belted Radial Whitewall

40,000 MILE LIMITED WARRANTY   **$33.95**

- Exceptional Handling

- Exceptional Traction

- 40,000 mile Limited Warranty

Ridgeway Import

Steel Belted Radial Blackwall

40,000 MILE LIMITED WARRANTY   **$28.95**

- Steel Belted SR Speed Rated

- 70 Series High Performance

- 40,000 mile Limited Warranty

Progress Check 6

Basics Practice

a. $\begin{array}{r} 10,375 \\ -\ 8,246 \\ \hline \end{array}$

b. $\begin{array}{r} 37.95 \\ \times\ \ \ 4 \\ \hline \end{array}$

c. $\begin{array}{r} 12,376 \\ +\ 7,500 \\ \hline \end{array}$

1. What kind of tire is the ad selling—radial, belted bias, or bias ply? Is this the type of tire that will last the longest?

2. Which is less expensive, the blackwall tire or the whitewall? How much less expensive?

3. Look again at the chart on page 229. How many more miles can you expect this tire to last than a bias-ply tire? How many more miles than a belted-bias tire?

4. What if you buy a radial tire and it lasts only 30,000 miles? How much less is that than promised by the warranty? Would you get all your money back for the tire? Why or why not?

Checking Car Clunks, Clanks, or Hums

Wordwise: You can take your car to a *diagnostic center* to find out what needs to be fixed. The people at the center don't do the repairs. They just check the car and give you advice.

When something doesn't sound right on your car, take it in to be checked. It is better than waiting and having a serious problem.

To find a good mechanic, ask others. Go to someone that others know is experienced and fair. Ask what it will cost to fix your car. Get the amount in writing. This is called an *estimate*. What you pay should be very close to the estimate. If it isn't, you have the right to complain. The mechanic should get your permission to make repairs that cost a lot more than the estimate.

Progress Check 7

Which estimate is closest to the actual cost—A, B, or C? How close? Write your answer on a separate piece of paper.

Estimate	Actual cost
A. $352.00	$450.00
B. $90.00	$86.24
C. $115.00	$113.90

How Do You Figure Out a Repair Bill?

Take a look at the repair bill on the facing page. Look at each part of it. At the top is information about the person whose car is being repaired. It also shows the mileage of the car, the date, and other information about the car. Read each item.

You will see what parts were needed to repair the car. The parts are listed on the left side. The work that is done is called *labor.* The labor is listed on the right where it says *Description of work.*

At the bottom of the repair bill you will see *Authorized by.* This means that the person who signed gave permission to do the repairs.

Progress Check 8

Write your answers on a separate piece of paper.

1. What kind of car is being repaired?

2. How many miles did the car have on it when it was brought in for repair?

3. Who authorized the work to be done?

4. How much of the repair bill was due to the cost of the parts? How much was labor? Which was the higher cost—parts or labor? How much higher?

5. How much was the tax on this job?

6. Suppose Rich Duggan paid cash for his car repairs. He gave Downtown Motor 3 fifty-dollar bills, 6 twenty-dollar bills, and 2 ten-dollar bills. How much change should he receive?

AMT.	NAME OF PART	SALE AMOUNT						

NAME *Rich Duggan*
ADDRESS *301 Apt. #14   Rollaway Drive*
CITY *Chicago*

AMT.	NAME OF PART	SALE AMOUNT	DATE *12/15/89*	ORDER NO.		WHEN PROMISED *12/17*	PHONE *555-2149*
1	Oil Filter	7 65	YEAR & MAKE OF CAR–TYPE OR MODEL *'82 Custom Corsair*		ESTIMATE *$235*	SERIAL NO.	
1	Fuel Filter	5 35				MOTOR NO.	
4	Spark Plugs	10 00					
	Brake Fluid	6 00	LICENSE NO. *999-LLK*		MILEAGE *108,795*	WRITTEN BY *Tom*	
1	Thermostat	4 85	DESCRIPTION OF WORK				AMOUNT
			Major Tune, Replace Fluids, Replace Thermostat				148 00
			Check Clutch System				
			Install Clutch Master				54 00
			Install Clutch Slave				36 00

	TOTAL PARTS 33 85	GAS, OIL & GREASE	CHECK BELOW		LABOR ONLY 238 00
ESTIMATES ARE FOR LABOR ONLY, MATERIAL ADDITIONAL.		LBS. GR.	LUBRICATE		PARTS 33 85
		GALS. GAS	ENGINE OIL		
		QTS. OIL 5 20/40 11 50	TRANS.		GAS, OIL & GREASE 11 50
		TOTAL GAS, OIL, & GREASE 11.50	TOTAL SERVICE		TAX 2 20
I HEREBY AUTHORIZE THE ABOVE REPAIR WORK TO BE DONE ALONG WITH NECESSARY MATERIALS.		AUTHORIZED BY *Rich Duggan*		TOTAL	285 55

Math on the Job

1. Kelly Driscoll sells car insurance. She has just sold a policy at the following premiums: liability—$512.48; medical payment—$110; uninsured motorist—$72; collision—$398.42; comprehensive—$153.50. What is the total premium for this policy?

2. Charlie Kray works for an insurance company. A client has come in with the following bills for damage to his car: $250 to fix a dent; $400 to replace a window; $150 to replace a dashboard; $498 to replace a car radio. The client has a $200 deductible on his policy. How much will Charlie authorize for the insurance company to pay?

3. Laurel Bryant is a traveling salesperson. This week, she drove the following amounts: Monday—253 miles; Tuesday—181 miles; Wednesday—94 miles; Thursday—123 miles; Friday—53 miles. What was her mileage for the week? What is the average amount of miles she travels per day? (total miles ÷ 5)

4. Jennifer Drake sells books for a publishing company. Last month she drove 2,262 miles for her company. They will pay her back $.18 per mile. What is the total amount she should put in her bill to them?

5. Ted Furokawa is a mechanic in a service station. The job he has just completed required the following parts: oil filter—$8; air filter—$9; spark plugs—$13.49; distributor cap—$16.82; spark plug wires—$26.78. What should he write down as the total cost for parts? If tax in his state is 7%, what is the total for parts?

6. Ted replaced five quarts of oil in the customer's car. Ted's station charges $1.98 per quart. Ted billed the customer $9.90 for oil. Did he figure the charge correctly?

7. Monica Lee writes down her odometer readings each time she uses her car for business. Look at her record for the week. How many miles each day can Monica charge toward business?

10/17	4855 to 4862
10/18	4865 to 4879
10/19	4892 to 4904
10/20	4913 to 4948
10/21	4951 to 5002

   How many miles did Monica drive on business for the entire week?

8. David Hoffman uses the company car to run business errands for his boss. Today the car was on empty so David filled the tank. The car took 15 gallons. The car had been driven 330 miles since the last time David filled the tank. David thinks the car might need a tune-up. It usually gets around 29 miles per gallon. What was the car's mileage this time? What's the difference between this amount and the car's normal mileage?

9. Rick took his car to the shop for a tune-up and an oil change. The parts cost $26.50. The total bill was $209.73. How much did Rick pay for labor?

Chapter Review

Chapter Summary

- Most car insurance includes five kinds of coverage. They are liability, medical payments, uninsured motorist, collision, and comprehensive.

- Basic insurance rates are not the same in all areas of the country. Where you live can make a difference in the amount of your premium.

- You can decide on your deductible. The deductible is the amount you agree to pay for damage or loss. The higher the deductible, the lower the premium.

- It pays to compare rates offered by different insurance companies. Make sure you get the lowest rate possible for the kind of insurance you need.

- Your odometer helps you figure your mileage. Keep track of the number of miles you travel in one month. Then multiply by 12 to estimate how many miles you'll drive in a year.

- To prevent car trouble, make sure to check your car's water and oil regularly. Take your car in for a check-up and oil change at least every 7,500 miles.

- The longest-lasting tire is a radial, which should last at least 40,000 miles.

- A repair estimate should be very close to the actual cost.

- A repair bill has two main kinds of costs—parts and labor.

- The person who will pay for the work must authorize the work to be done.

Chapter Quiz

Write your answers on a separate sheet of paper.

1. An insurance policy will usually cover liability, medical payments, uninsured motorist, collision, and _____.

2. The insurance company pays the cost of collision damage after you pay the amount of the _____.

3. Your odometer reads 31,982 on January 1. On February 1, it reads 33,001. How many miles did you travel in one month?

4. A belted bias tire is good for 25,000 miles. A radial is good for 40,000 miles. How much longer would you expect the radial to last?

5. Which of these estimates is the closest to the actual cost?

Estimate A:	$132.78	Actual Cost:	$178.23
Estimate B:	$90.00	Actual Cost:	$97.90
Estimate C:	$322.00	Actual Cost:	$406.17

   Which estimate is the furthest from the actual cost? How far off is it?

6. You pay $144.62 for car repair. You give the cashier 6 twenty-dollar bills and 3 ten-dollar bills. How much change will you receive?

7. You park your car in a lot. When you come back, your new stereo has been stolen from your car. You paid $497 for it. Your comprehensive deductible is $100. How much do you expect the insurance company to pay for the theft of your stereo?

Challenge

Get a map of the United States that has a key showing distance. Find out about how many miles you would travel to get from where you are now to Port Angeles, Washington. Imagine that your car's odometer reads 49,782 today. How many miles would be on it if you went to and from Port Angeles?

Unit Seven Review

Answer the questions below. Look back at Chapters 13 and 14 if you need help.

1. What are four things you should think about before buying a car?

2. What is the Blue Book?

3. What is meant by *high-book* and *low-book* prices?

4. When you find a car you think might be right, what are three of the things you should do?

5. What is a finance charge?

6. Where can you find the best deals on car loans?

7. What are five kinds of insurance coverage you will probably need?

8. What are three things that might affect how much you pay for insurance?

9. How often should you check your car's oil and water? How often will your car need an oil change?

10. What two main kinds of costs are listed on a repair bill?

Unit Eight

Cash or Credit

15 Credit Card Math

Careless use of credit cards can ruin your budget. What should you think about before you use a credit card?

Chapter Learning Objectives

- List three good things and three bad things about having a credit card.
- Fill out an application for a credit account.
- Figure out a bill on a credit account.
- Compare saving and borrowing to buy expensive items.
- Figure simple and compound interest on savings.
- Review basic math skills in the Appendix at the back of this textbook.

Words to Know

credit card a card that allows you to buy things without using cash

co-applicant a person who applies with another person for a service or privilege

compound interest interest on the principal (money in a savings account) and on the interest already earned

principal money in a savings account or owed on a bill, not counting interest

simple interest interest on the principal only

Credit Cards—Good or Bad?

Just about everywhere you go, **credit cards** are being used—in stores, gas stations, restaurants, and hotels. In fact, there aren't very many things you can't buy with a credit card. But is using a card a good idea?

Did You Know?
VISA and MasterCard are accepted by about four million businesses in the United States.

Here are some of the good things about having a credit card:

1. You can buy something you want now and pay for it later.
2. You don't have to carry a lot of cash with you.
3. You can purchase things over the telephone.
4. Your credit card bill is a record of your purchases.
5. You will have a way to pay for something in an emergency.

Here are some of the bad things:

1. You may buy more than you can afford since you don't need cash to do it.

2. You'll have to pay interest on the amount you owe on your account. (This amount is called your *unpaid balance.*)

3. You may have to pay an annual fee of from $15.00 to $40.00.

How Do Interest Rates Work?

Here's a Tip: Pay attention to the interest rate charges on credit card bills. Compare rates from time to time. If you can pay less elsewhere, consider switching credit card companies.

Unless you pay your bill within 25 to 30 days, you'll usually pay interest on what you owe. The interest rates will differ depending on the card you get. They'll usually range from 15% to 22% per year. This means you'll pay an annual finance charge of 15% to 22% on your unpaid balance.

Calculator Practice

If the annual (yearly) interest rate is 18%, how much is the monthly interest rate?

Enter .18

Press ÷

Enter 12 (12 months in a year)

Press =

Your answer should be: .015 or $1\frac{1}{2}$ % interest.

Suppose you buy school or work clothes using a credit card. The total price of the clothes is $220. The store's interest rate is 18%. You pay $20 of the $220 on your first month's bill. What you still owe will not be just $200. You will owe $200 plus the finance charge. This would be $3.

Progress Check 1

Write your answers on a separate piece of paper.

Basics Practice

a. .08 x $639.00 = ?

b. .21 x $200.00 = ?

c. $288.00 ÷ 12 = ?

1. Jill buys these items from a department store: a lamp for $39.90 and a stereo for $499. The store adds 6% sales tax. What is the total amount she owes?

2. Jill charges the lamp and the stereo. Then she pays $30 on her first month's credit-card bill. What is the unpaid balance?

3. The interest rate on Jill's credit card is 24% a year. How much interest is that per month? (Remember, a year has 12 months.)

4. What will Jill's bill be the second month?

Solve It

a. What is Jill's unpaid balance? (Insert answer to question 2: _____)

b. What is the monthly interest? (Insert answer to question 3: _____)

c. What is the total of unpaid balance and monthly interest? (Add the answers to a and b.)

5. Suppose you buy on credit from a store with an interest rate of 18%. You must pay a finance charge only if your bill is not paid in full within 25 days. On April 2, you buy a belt for $23.78. On April 24, you pay $23.78 on your bill. What will be the finance charge on your next billing statement?

How Does Charging Compare to Saving?

When you buy any item on credit, you pay more for it if you have to pay interest.

Here's a Tip: It's important to have a minimum of three months' salary saved in case you're laid off or need to change jobs.

Suppose you pay 21% interest on your credit account and you have $650 worth of charges. Your interest for the month is $11.38.

Now imagine you saved $650 to buy what you needed. You kept it in a savings account for one month at an interest rate of 5.25%. You earned $2.84 in **simple interest**. You also did not have to pay the $11.38 interest you would have paid if you bought on credit.

What is the total amount you saved?

Solve It

$ 2.84	interest earned by saving
+ 11.38	interest you didn't have to pay
?	amount saved

The longer you leave savings in an account, the more it earns. You earn interest on the money you deposit. Sometimes you earn interest on your interest, too. This is called **compound interest.** It can be figured once a year, twice a year (semi-annually), every three months (quarterly), or every day (daily). Suppose you save $300 for a year at an interest rate of 6%. (Remember, 6% is the same as .06.) It is compounded quarterly. At the end of three months, your new balance is $300 plus $4.50 in interest.

So $304.50 is your balance at the end of the first quarter. In the second quarter, you'll earn interest on your original deposit of $300 (the **principal**). You'll also earn interest on the $4.50. To figure compound interest, you need to follow these steps:

They're Not All the Same: The more often interest is compounded, the more you earn. The reason for this is that you earn interest on your interest.

1. Multiply the principal by the interest by the time period. (If it's quarterly, multiply by .25. If it's semi-annually, multiply by .5. If it's annually, multiply by 1.)

2. Add the interest to the principal.
3. Multiply the new total by the interest by the time period.

Solve It

$300 x .06 x .25 = $4.50

$300 + $4.50 = $304.50

$304.50 x .06 x .25 = _____ compound interest

Basics Practice

Change these percentages to decimals.

a.   4% = ?

b. $5\frac{1}{2}$% = ?

c. $6\frac{3}{4}$% = ?

d.   14% = ?

Progress Check 2

Write your answers on a separate piece of paper.

1. You deposit $200 at an annual interest rate of $5\frac{1}{2}$ % compounded quarterly. What amount of interest will you earn for the first quarter? ($200 x .055 x .25 = ?)
2. Add your principal of $200 and your interest (answer to question 1) to find your new balance.
3. Multiply your new balance (answer to question 2) by the interest rate (.055) by .25. What is your compounded interest at the end of the second quarter?

Applying for a Credit Card

Suppose you decide you want a credit card. You can get an application from a bank or store that offers the card.

Some cards are for one purpose, like buying gas or charging phone calls. Other cards are for many purposes. They may be travel and entertainment cards or bank credit cards.

You can use the card in place of cash at any place that accepts your credit card.

Here is an application for a department store credit card. Notice the kinds of information that you are asked to fill in. If you're married, you might want a joint account that both you and your spouse can use. You would then need to give information about your spouse, the **co-applicant.**

Gunn's Department Store Credit Card Application

❶ TYPE OF ACCOUNT REQUESTED (CHECK ONE): ☐ INDIVIDUAL ☐ JOINT
(Married applicants may apply for separate accounts)

❷ FIRST NAME INITIAL LAST NAME

HOME ADDRESS APT.# CITY STATE ZIP

❸ ☐ RENT ☐ WITH PARENTS HOW LONG? HOME Include Area Code
☐ OWN ☐ BOARD YRS. PHONE

DATE OF BIRTH SOCIAL SECURITY NO. DRIVER'S LICENSE NO.—STATE

❹ PREVIOUS ADDRESS — If less than 2 years at current CITY STATE / ZIP

❺ EMPLOYER POSITION HOW LONG?
YRS.

BUSINESS ADDRESS BUSINESS PHONE Include Area Code

FORMER EMPLOYER — If less than 2 years at current

❻ CO-APPLICANT INFORMATION (if Joint Account requested)
FIRST NAME INITIAL LAST NAME RELATIONSHIP TO SOCIAL
APPLICANT (if any) SECURITY NO.

EMPLOYER EMPLOYER'S ADDRESS POSITION HOW LONG?

❼ BANK— LIST BRANCH AND ADDRESS ☐ CHECKING
☐ SAVINGS

OTHER CREDIT REFERENCES? ACCOUNT NO.

Progress Check 3

Write your answers on a separate piece of paper.

1. Suppose you have lived in your roommate's apartment for 18 months. What would you write on line 4?

2. Suppose you have lived there for 2 years and 3 months. What would you write on line 4?

3. Suppose you have had your present job for a year and 9 months. What would you write on the last line of section 5?

4. Suppose you have had your present job for almost 3 years. What would you write on the last line of section 5?

5. Suppose you have worked at your present job for exactly 48 months. In section 5, what would you put in the box that asks "How long?"

Reading a Credit-Card Bill

Each time you buy something with your credit card, you get a receipt. Look at the receipt to make sure it has the correct price of the item you're buying. Then sign the receipt and keep your copy. The store uses its copy of the receipt to figure your bill. Then the store mails you a billing statement. You use your receipts when you check your billing statement.

Here's a Tip:
Sign the credit card as soon as you get it. Put it away after you use it. Don't leave it lying around. Treat it like cash.

Here's the way to do it:

1. Compare your receipts and the billing statement. Be certain you've been billed correctly.

2. Make sure any payments you made have been credited to your account.

3. If you returned anything, make sure the refund has been credited to your account.

4. Look to see how much you owe and when it's due.

5. Look to see how much credit you have left in your account. A credit limit is the maximum amount you can charge.

Read this portion of a bill. Notice that there have been no new charges for purchases. A payment of $50 has been credited to the account.

PREVIOUS BALANCE	CHARGES	FINANCE CHARGE	CREDIT/ RETURNS	PAYMENTS	NEW BALANCE	PAST DUE AMOUNT
247.07	.00	3.59	.00	50.00	200.66	.00

ACCOUNT NO.	CREDIT LIMIT	TO AVOID ADDITIONAL **FINANCE CHARGE**, PAY BALANCE IN FULL BY DUE DATE NOTED ➡		PAYMENT DUE DATE	MINIMUM PAYMENT DUE
999-888	800			08-23-89	20.00

Progress Check 4

Here's a Tip: When you pay a bill, you should write your account number on the front of your check. This will help make sure that the payment is credited to your account, and not to somebody else's.

Write your answers on a separate piece of paper.

1. What is the number of this account?
2. When is the payment due?
3. What is the credit limit on the account?
4. What is the new balance? How much more can be charged on the account before the credit limit is reached?
5. What is the amount of credits and returns?
6. What is the amount of the finance charge?
7. What is the amount owed? What is the minimum payment due?

What Is an Annual Fee?

An annual fee is the amount charged yearly by the credit card company or bank. You'll usually pay from $15 to $40 a year. This amount is charged to your account. If you pay an annual fee of $30, that's $2.50 a month (30 ÷ 12 months).

Progress Check 5

1. Suppose you have a credit card that charges an annual fee of $40. If you figured the annual fee per month, how much would it cost monthly?

2. Imagine you apply for a card so you can pay for a computer. The computer costs $1,295. The annual fee on your new card is $40. You pay $200 down on the computer and you put the rest on your credit account. How much do you owe as soon as you open your account?

Should You Buy on Credit?

How do you know when buying on credit is not for you? Ask yourself these questions:

- Are the payments for my credit debts below 20% of my net monthly pay?
- Do I have some cash saved?
- Am I able to get a credit account paid up if I try?

Would you answer "no" to any of these questions? If so, don't buy on credit.

Progress Check 6

Write your answers on a separate piece of paper.

1. Suppose your net pay is $1,075 a month. Your total credit payments average $215 a month. What percentage of your net pay are your debts? Should you stop buying on credit?

Calculator Practice

Enter 215

Press ÷

Enter 1075

Press =

Your answer should be: .20 or 20%

2. Rhonda's net pay is $882 a month. Her credit payments are $60. What percentage of Rhonda's pay are her debts?

3. Ernie has $610.47 saved. He has to get his car repaired for $447. What will he have remaining in his savings? He wants to replace the $447 over the next six months. How much should he deposit in his savings account each month?

Should You Borrow?

Sometimes you can borrow cash with your credit card. The loan can be an *instant loan* of $50 to $100. Or it may be $500 to $5,000, depending on your credit record. It's tempting to get quick cash, but you'll usually pay very high interest rates. If you borrow $1,000 at 22% interest per year, what would the interest be for a year?

Calculator Practice

Enter 1000

Press x

Enter .22 (for 22%)

Press =

Your interest for a year should be: $220

Whenever you consider a quick loan, make sure to stop and figure the total amount you could pay.

Before buying any big item on credit, ask yourself this question: Will the item still be usable when I have finally finished paying for it?

Progress Check 7

Write your answers on a separate piece of paper.

1. You borrow $800 at an interest rate of 19%. What will the interest charge be for that year?
2. You borrow $500 at an interest rate of 21%. What will the interest charge be for one year?

Math on the Job

1. Wally Washington is a billing clerk at the Appliance Corral. A customer bought a $500 refrigerator on a store credit account. Appliance Corral charges 19% interest. What finance charge will Wally enter on the first month's bill? ($500 x .19 = yearly interest. Yearly interest ÷ 12 = finance charge for one month.)

2. Susanna Rainfeather handles complaints at Chairs Galore. A customer wants to pay only occasionally on her charge account. Susanna explains that the store's credit policy requires a minimum monthly payment of 5%. The customer's unpaid balance is $432. How much will Susanna advise the customer to pay?

Chapter Review

Chapter Summary

- Credit cards allow you to buy something now and pay for it later.

- Credit cards can be risky. They make it easy to spend more than you can afford.

- If you don't pay the whole credit card bill right away, you will be charged interest on the unpaid balance. You will probably also pay an annual fee for the credit card.

- When you buy on credit, you might pay more for the item than it actually costs. This is because interest charges are added to the unpaid balance.

- In a savings account, simple interest is paid on the principal only. Compound interest is paid on the principal plus the interest already earned.

- When you apply for a credit card, you need to fill out an application. Then the bank or store that issues the card has to approve the application.

- It's important to keep track of your debts. If your credit debt is more than 20% of your net pay, it is not a good idea to buy more on credit.

- When you borrow, you should calculate how much you'll have to pay back. Total repayment includes the interest on the amount you borrowed.

Chapter Quiz

Write your answers on a separate sheet of paper.

1. Name three good things and three bad things about having a credit card.

2. Imogen purchased clothes using a credit card. Her purchases totaled $216. Right away, she paid $25 toward the credit card bill. The interest rate on her credit card is 21%. How much will the monthly finance charge be on the next bill Imogen gets?

3. Which of these describes compound interest?
   a. interest paid on the total of the principal plus interest already earned on the principal
   b. interest paid on the principal alone
   c. annual fees for a credit card

4. Sam's net pay is $895 per month. The total of his credit payments is $95 per month. What percentage of Sam's net pay are his credit debts?

5. If your credit limit is $600 and your charges are $222.14, how much more are you allowed to buy on credit?

6. Ken's purchases on February 5 come to $111.34. On February 26, a payment is due. What amount does Ken need to pay to keep from having to pay a finance charge?

Challenge

Find out the interest rates on credit accounts at three large stores in your area. Write each finance charge next to the store's name. Where would you pay the highest charge on an unpaid balance? Where would you pay the lowest charge?

16 Loans and Interest

You can apply for a bank loan if you have an emergency or need to make a large purchase.

Chapter Learning Objectives

- Fill out an application for a personal bank loan.
- List characteristics of a good and bad credit rating.
- Interpret a promissory note.
- Define fixed interest and variable interest.
- Figure interest on loans of varying amounts and lengths.
- Review basic math skills in the Appendix at the back of this textbook.

Words to Know

collateral   something used as security for a loan

cosigner   someone who signs a loan contract with a borrower and promises to pay if the borrower doesn't pay

dividend   money earned as profit by a company and divided among people who invested money in the company

fixed interest rate   a percentage that doesn't change

lien   a claim on property or possessions for payment of a debt

promissory note   a written promise to pay back a loan or money you owe

qualify   to show you are able to take on a responsibility, job, or task

variable interest rate   a percentage that changes or varies

verification   proof of the truth

Getting a Loan from a Bank

They're Not All the Same: All banks do not have the same terms for loans. Shop for good loans as you would for a car or an insurance policy.

Someday you may need to get a loan for personal use. You may need extra money to pay a debt. You may need extra money to pay first and last months' rent on a new apartment. Or you may need extra money for an emergency, such as car repairs. If so, you'll need to go through these steps to get a loan:

1. Go to the bank and fill out an application form.
2. Present any needed **verifications** of income, such as pay stubs or tax returns.

3. After approval of your credit, review and sign the loan contract.

4. Pay a loan fee.

What's on a Loan Application?

On the facing page is a sample loan application. Read each item.

Progress Check 1

Write your answers on a separate piece of paper.

1. Look at Section A. Gloria wants to borrow $2,400 for two years. What will she write on the line before the word *months?* (Remember, a year has 12 months.)

2. Look at Section B. Jim has lived at his current address for 30 months. Will he have to fill out any information under *Previous Address?*

3. Look at Section C. Stan has been working at the cycle shop for 26 months. What will he put in the boxes on the third line?

4. Fran is a waitress. She works 140 hours a month and earns $4.50 an hour in pay. What would she put on line 1 in Section D?

5. Fran owns some shares in a company she helped to start ten years ago. She is paid $50 a month in **dividends** from this investment. She also earns $44 a month on a savings account of $8,000. What would she put on line 2 in Section D?

6. Fran's tips average $9.50 an hour. What would she put on line 3 in Section D?

7. What would Fran put on line 4 in Section D?

Consumer Loan Application

YOUR CREDIT REQUEST

A

WHAT DO YOU WANT THIS LOAN FOR?_____

LOAN: $_____ FOR _____ MONTHS ☐ FIXED INTEREST RATE   (Explain Purpose)
☐ CAPPED VARIABLE INTEREST RATE

MARITAL STATUS   ☐ MARRIED   ☐ UNMARRIED   ☐ SEPARATED

THIS APPLICATION IS ☐ IN YOUR NAME ALONE   ☐ JOINTLY WITH _____

If applying jointly, each of you must complete a separate application.

YOURSELF

B

FIRST NAME	MIDDLE INITIAL	LAST NAME

CURRENT ADDRESS   STREET   APT. NO.   TIME THERE
                                                            YRS.   MOS.

CITY   STATE   ZIP CODE   ☐ OWN   ☐ RENT
                                                ☐ I LIVE WITH PARENTS

PREVIOUS ADDRESS   STREET   APT. NO.   TIME THERE
(if at current address less than three years)   YRS.   MOS.

CITY   STATE   ZIP CODE   DATE OF BIRTH

SOCIAL SECURITY NO.   DRIVER'S LICENSE NO.

HOME PHONE NO.   DEPENDENTS OTHER THAN SELF OR SPOUSE

BEST TIME TO CALL YOU   BEST PLACE TO CALL YOU
☐ MORNING ☐ AFTERNOON ☐ EVENING   ☐ HOME   ☐ WORK

NEAREST RELATIVE/FRIEND NOT LIVING WITH YOU   RELATIONSHIP   PHONE No.

ADDRESS   STREET   CITY   STATE   ZIP CODE

YOUR EMPLOYMENT

C

CURRENT EMPLOYER   WORK PHONE NO.

EMPLOYER'S ADDRESS   CITY   STATE   ZIP CODE

TIME THERE   OCCUPATION
☐ YRS.   ☐ MOS.

PREVIOUS EMPLOYER (if with current employer OCCUPATION   TIME THERE
                    less than three years)   YRS.   MOS.

EMPLOYER'S ADDRESS   CITY   STATE   ZIP CODE

YOUR INCOME

D

MONTHLY GROSS SALARY AND WAGES	$
DIVIDENDS AND INTEREST	$
OTHER INCOME (DESCRIBE)	$
YOUR MONTHLY INCOME	$

Below is Section E of the loan application. This part asks for information about your bank accounts.

YOUR BANKING RELATIONSHIPS			
TYPE OF ACCOUNT	FINANCIAL INSTITUTION	ACCOUNT #	BALANCE
CHECKING			
SAVINGS			
OTHER (SPECIFY)			

Progress Check 2

1. Christine has a checking account at the Bank of Billions. Her checking account number is 1182-6609. Her balance is $63.04. How would she fill out the first line in Section E?

2. Christine also has a savings account at First Avenue Bank. Her account number is 4567-891023. Her balance is $826.38. How would she fill out the second line in Section E?

How Does the Bank Use Your Loan Application?

A loan officer at the bank takes your application. That person also collects any other papers requested from you, such as tax forms. Then the loan officer checks on these things:

- the place of your employment and your income.
- your credit history.

The loan officer needs to know if you **qualify** for a loan. You need to prove that you have good credit and will be able to repay the loan.

What Do You Need for a Good Credit Rating?

To get a good credit rating, it is important for you to have:

- a steady job.
- a credit history that shows you pay your bills on time.
- a checking or savings account.

What Can Prevent You from Getting a Loan?

There are some things that can work against you when you apply for a loan. Ask yourself these questions:

1. Do I have some way to identify myself? Do I have a driver's license, a Social Security card, a draft card, or a birth certificate?
2. Do I have a permanent address (one that isn't in a hotel, in care of someone else, or at a post office box)?
3. Have I been a *job hopper*, or have I held a steady job?
4. Am I going into the armed services before I can repay the loan?
5. Am I under 21? (Younger persons may need to get a **cosigner**.)
6. Has a **lien** ever been put on anything I own?
7. Have any of my bills been turned over to a collection agency?
8. Am I past due with a payment on any account?

Here's a Tip: It's risky to be a cosigner. Don't do it unless you can trust the person to pay. Otherwise, you'll have to pay off the loan.

Correcting a Bad Credit Rating

If you have a bad credit rating, you can change it. This is what you have to do:

- Pay every one of your bills.
- Use **collateral** to get an installment loan. Then pay the loan in full, making payments on time.
- Get an account at a department store. Charge only in small amounts that you pay promptly.

What's in a Report from a Credit Bureau?

People who work for a credit bureau get information about any buying you do on credit. They find out about any charge accounts you have. They keep a record of any loans you have taken out.

A credit report will usually include this kind of information:

1. The date you opened your account at a particular store or business.
2. The number of your account.
3. The dates of your purchases and payments.
4. The highest amount you have owed in the past on this account.
5. Your credit limit on the account.
6. The amount of your current balance.
7. Any amount that is past due.
8. Any time-payment loan you have.

9. The way you're paying the loan—on what terms and how fast.
10. Court actions against you, or current problems with creditors.

Progress Check 3

Write your answers on a separate piece of paper.

1. Name three documents you could use to identify yourself.

2. Which address will make you seem most reliable?
   a. a post office box
   b. a street address and apartment number
   c. a house address in care of a friend

3. The balance in your department store account is $200.66. Last month the minimum payment due was $19. The month before it was $15. You've made no payment for 60 days. Today you paid $30. Is your payment on this account past due?

Completing the Paperwork

Imagine that your credit has been checked. The loan officer at the bank says your loan has been approved. You need to go in and do the paperwork. This means you'll go over some papers with the loan officer and review the terms of your contract. At some banks, one of the papers you'll need to sign is a **promissory note**. On the next page is the way one kind of promissory note looks.

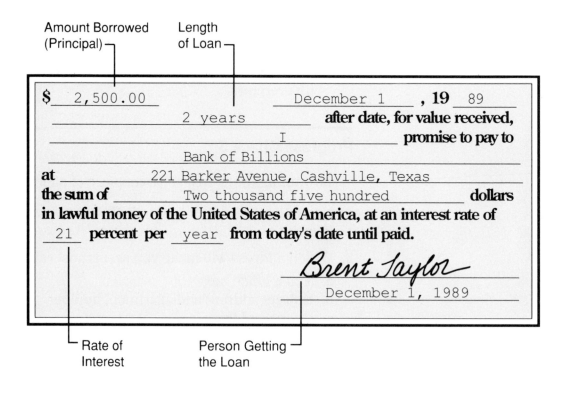

Amount Borrowed (Principal)

Length of Loan

$ 2,500.00   December 1 , 19 89

2 years   **after date, for value received,**

I   **promise to pay to**

Bank of Billions

at 221 Barker Avenue, Cashville, Texas

the sum of Two thousand five hundred **dollars**

in lawful money of the United States of America, at an interest rate of

21 **percent per** year **from today's date until paid.**

Brent Taylor

December 1, 1989

Rate of Interest

Person Getting the Loan

Basics Practice

a. $2,400 x .22 = ?

b. $2,400
    + 528

c. $81.33
    x 36

Progress Check 4

Read each item on the promissory note. Then write your answers on a separate piece of paper.

1. Who is getting the loan?
2. Who is the lender (person or company giving the loan)?
3. How much money is being loaned?
4. What is the interest rate on the loan?
5. How long does the borrower have to repay the loan?
6. In what city and state was the money loaned?
7. On what date was it signed by the borrower?
8. How much can the borrower expect to pay in interest alone?

$2,500	(loan amount)
x .21	(interest rate)
?	(interest for one year)
x 2	(length of time)
?	(interest for two years)

9. Add the amount borrowed (principal) to the interest. How much will be paid to the bank altogether?

10. Suppose the note is for $3,200 at 16% interest for one year. How much will be repaid altogether?

What Interest Do You Pay?

The interest rate on a personal loan will almost always be fixed. A **fixed interest rate** is one unchanging percentage. A **variable interest rate** is one that can change. For example, the rate might be at $16\frac{3}{4}$% at first. Then it may go up to 17% in six months. Then it could move up again. Usually there is a limit (called a *cap*). The cap is the most an interest rate can go up to once you've got the loan.

Solve It

1. Suppose you have a loan with an interest rate of $17\frac{1}{4}$%. The interest rate is variable. It can vary only $2\frac{1}{2}$%. How high can your interest rate go?

$$17\frac{1}{4} \quad = \quad 17\frac{1}{4}$$
$$+ \ 2\frac{1}{2} \quad = \quad 2\frac{2}{4}$$
$$\overline{\qquad\qquad\qquad}$$
$$= \text{ Highest Interest}$$

2. Suppose you have a fixed interest loan. It is for $1,000 at an interest rate of 19%. How much would you pay in interest per year?

Calculator Practice

Enter 1000

Press x

Enter .19

Press =

Your interest for a year should be: $190

The chart below shows four different loans. Each one is in a different amount at a different interest rate.

Loan Number	Principal	Rate of Interest	Length of Loan
1	$1,500	18%	Two Years
2	2,500	21.25%	Two Years
3	900	20%	One Year
4	3,000	22%	Three Years

Progress Check 5

Write your answers on a separate piece of paper. How much must be repaid altogether for each of the loans listed above? Use the steps shown in the Calculator Practice on page 265 to figure the total amounts for each loan.

Calculator Practice

Here is how to use your calculator to figure the answer for Loan Number 1.

Step 1:
Enter 1500 (principal)
Press x
Enter .18 (rate of interest)

Press x
Enter 2 (length of loan)
Press = 540 (interest for two years)

Step 2:
Enter 1500 (principal)
Press +
Enter 540 (interest for two years)
Press = 2040 (total amount to be repaid)

What's a Loan Fee?

At the time you get your loan money, you'll need to pay a loan fee. You can have it taken out of the amount you're borrowing. Or you can pay for it with cash or a check.

Suppose the loan fee for a bank loan is $55. The loan is for $1,200. What will be left if the loan fee is deducted from the loan?

Solve It

$1,200   amount of loan
 − 55   loan fee
 ?   amount left after loan fee is deducted

Progress Check 6

Write your answers on a separate piece of paper.

1. What is a cosigner?
2. What is a fixed interest rate?
3. What is a variable interest rate?
4. Which of the following does *qualifying for a loan* mean?

   a. meeting the requirements for receiving the loan
   b. having a large debt
   c. filling out a loan application

Basics Practice

a. $2,000 x .18 = ?

b.
$$\begin{array}{r} \$2,000 \\ + 360 \\ \hline \end{array}$$

c.
$$\begin{array}{r} \$2,360 \\ + 55 \\ \hline \end{array}$$

Math on the Job

1. Joe Mellis is a plumber. He's borrowing $1,200 to pay first and last months' payments on a new lease. His interest rate is 20%. He plans to pay back the loan in a year by working extra hours. At $45 an hour, how many extra hours will Joe need? ($1,200 x .20 = interest. Interest + $1,200 = total. Total ÷ $45 = number of hours.)

2. Loni Lesh is a billing clerk at Blort's Specialty Store. Blort's requires a 5% minimum monthly payment on credit accounts. A customer with an unpaid balance of $416.88 has made a payment of $18 this month. Will Laura find that the customer has made the minimum payment? ($416.88 x .05 = minimum payment due)

3. Christina Allgood is a farmer. She needs a new pickup truck. A three-year loan will cost $210 a month or $2,520 per year. Christina's crops bring in $19,000 net per year. She doesn't want to spend more than 15% of her net income for the truck payments. Can she afford the loan?

4. Robert Karshouf does word processing at home. Robert needs a loan to buy a new, faster laser printer. The printer will cost $2,500, but it will add $320 a month to his income. He wants to pay off the loan in one year using his added $320 a month. At 21% interest, can Robert afford the monthly payments (Loan + interest = total. Total ÷ 12 = ?)

5. Claudia Alden is a data processing clerk at the Two Guys Finance Company. Claudia calculates monthly finance charges on customer loans. A customer has just made a payment of $170 on an unpaid loan balance of $1,325. The interest rate is 22%. What finance charge will Claudia post for next month? (New balance x .22 = interest. Interest ÷ 12 = finance charge.)

6. Mark is going to buy a new car. The sticker price on the car is $22,500. He is going to pay 11% interest over 3 years. Find his monthly payment. (Cost of car x .11 = interest; cost of car + interest divided by number of payments.)

Chapter Review

Chapter Summary

- The first step toward getting a bank loan is to fill out an application form.

- The bank checks on your employment, your income, and your credit history.

- To get a good credit rating, it's important for you to do three things:

  a. have a steady job.
  b. pay your bills on time.
  c. have a checking or savings account.

- To correct a bad credit rating, first you need to pay all your bills.

- A credit bureau gets information about any buying you do on credit. It also has a record of any loans you've taken out.

- A fixed interest rate is unchanging. A variable interest rate can change.

- To figure the amount of interest on a loan, you multiply the principal by the interest rate by the length of the loan.

- A promissory note is one of the papers you may need to sign to get a loan. The note is your written promise to pay back the loan. Both the amount of time and interest rate are shown on the note.

- You will need to pay a loan fee for getting a bank loan.

Chapter Quiz

Write your answers on a separate sheet of paper.

1. What is a changing interest rate called?

2. What is an unchanging interest rate called?

3. Figure the amounts that will be repaid to the bank on the following loans:

	Principal	Rate of Interest	Length of Loan
a.	$2,200.00	18.5%	One Year
b.	500.00	21%	Six Months
c.	3,000.00	20%	Two Years

4. When you go to the bank for a loan, what do you need to fill out?

5. Name three things that are checked before your loan application is approved.

6. Name three types of identification you could use to prove who you are.

7. What is a cosigner?

8. Name two ways to correct a bad credit rating.

Challenge

Create a promissory note for an invented person. Use the promissory note on page 262 as an example. The lender can be the Bank of Billions. Fill in the amount, the length of the loan, and the interest rate. Also, figure the cost of repaying the loan. Write that amount on the bottom. Label it *Total Amount to Be Repaid.*

Unit Eight Review

Read the questions. Write the answers on a separate piece of paper.

1. What are the four steps you must go through to get a loan?

2. What are three good things about having a credit card? What are three bad things about having a credit card?

3. What happens if you leave savings in an account for a long time?

4. Before you buy on credit, what three questions should you ask yourself?

5. Why is it usually not a good idea to borrow using your credit card?

6. What are two things you could do to correct a bad credit rating?

7. Name five things that could work against a person who wanted a loan.

8. What is a promissory note?

9. What is one thing that can happen if you are late with a bank payment?

10. What does a credit bureau do?

Unit Nine

Recreation, Travel, and Entertainment

17 Budgeting for Recreation

Even hiking costs money if you need equipment. How much should you budget for recreation?

Chapter Learning Objectives

- Identify three kinds of costs for recreational activities.
- Estimate costs of various activities, including equipment and clothing.
- Compare differing costs for the same activity.
- List equipment and clothing that might be needed for an activity.
- Interpret a chart.
- Review basic math skills in the Appendix at the back of this textbook.

Words to Know

estimate   a quick, but not exact judgment; a good guess about how many or how much

spectator sport   a sport, or athletic event, that has spectators, or people, who watch but don't take part

inventory   a list of supplies, equipment, or merchandise

Why Budget for Recreation?

Some of the things you most enjoy doing in your spare time may be free or almost free. You may like watching television, riding a bicycle, running, or reading. But what if your favorite activities aren't free? What if you enjoy working out at a gym, taking piano or flute lessons, or swimming at a public pool? If you plan for the expense, you'll look forward to it even more. And you'll be able to relax and have more fun in your spare time.

How Do You Figure Costs?

Did You Know?
Sometimes bowling alleys have special discounts. For example, some nights the cost might be $5 an hour for as many games as you want.

You can plan for the expense of any kind of recreation. Just ask yourself these questions:

1. How much does the actual activity cost? (For example, bowling might cost $1.95 a game.)
2. What will it cost to rent any equipment or clothes I need? (It may cost $1 to rent bowling shoes.)
3. What else might I pay for while I'm doing this? (Popcorn and a soft drink at a bowling alley may cost $2.10.)

By asking and answering these questions, you should be able to **estimate** your costs. Then you'll know how much you need to budget to enjoy your favorite activity.

Take a look at the costs at Valleyville Bowl.

Welcome to Valleyville Bowl

9 A.M. – 5 P.M.:	$2.00 per person per game
5 P.M. – 10 P.M.:	$2.15 per person per game
Juniors (under 18)	
Weekdays 9–5:	$1.25 per person per game
Shoe rental:	$1.00 per pair.

Sometimes the time of the activity changes the cost. Notice that there are different prices for different times at Valleyville Bowl.

Solve It

Look at the sign for Valleyville Bowl. Suppose you're 19 years old. How much will you save by bowling four games before 5:00 P.M. instead of from 6:30 to 8:00 P.M.?

$$\begin{array}{r} \$2.15 \\ -\,2.00 \\ \hline \end{array}$$
$$\times\,4 = ?$$

Progress Check 1

Write your answers on a separate piece of paper.

1. Your brother is celebrating his fifteenth birthday. He wants to take three friends bowling. All of his friends are his age. They play three games before

5:00 P.M. Your brother pays for the games and buys soft drinks at 90¢ each for four people. His guests pay for their own shoes. How much money does your brother pay for the afternoon?

2. Suppose you're over 18. You and one friend will bowl two games at 7:00 P.M. You'll pay for the games and for shoe rental. You want to have money left to buy pizza, which will cost about $10.50. How much do you estimate the evening will cost altogether? How much will it cost to do this three times a month?

How Do You Budget for Lessons?

Suppose you want to take some kind of lessons in your spare time. There are lots of different kinds to choose from. You might take horn or drum lessons, singing lessons, or even skydiving lessons. You might want to speak another language or do creative writing. You might want to learn how to box or how to be a chef. You can find a teacher for almost anything.

Progress Check 2

Write your answers on a separate piece of paper.

1. You decide to take guitar lessons. Each one-hour lesson costs $20. How much will you budget to pay for a one-hour lesson each week for 26 weeks? How much for a year, or 52 weeks?

2. Your sister and her best friend are going to take tap-dancing lessons once a week. They will pay $15 each for each lesson. They plan to take 12 lessons. How much does each person need to save for the 12 lessons? How much will they pay together?

3. Your sister's shoes will cost $48 a pair. What will be her total expense for lessons and shoes?

How Do You Budget for Spectator Sports?

A **spectator sport** is one that involves watching. But sometimes watching gets pretty expensive. To go to a game or other sport may cost more than you first imagine. It's important to ask yourself these questions when you're thinking about the extras:

- Will I need to pay to park my car?
- Will I need to pay for public transportation to get there?
- Will I buy a program?
- Will I buy something to eat or drink?
- Will I rent a cushion or a pair of binoculars?

Progress Check 3

Write your answers on a separate piece of paper.

1. Suppose that you're going to a baseball game. The ticket is $15. It will cost you $2.50 to park your car near the stadium. You will buy something to eat while you're at the game. You've saved $27 for the whole event. After you buy your ticket and pay to park your car, what will you have left to spend?

2. You are taking a friend to the stock car races. Each ticket is $7. A program costs $1.25. Hot dogs are $2, and drinks are $1.50. You buy two tickets, two programs, two hot dogs, and two drinks to share with your friend. How much do you spend? How much should you budget if you want to do this twice a month?

Save on Bargain Days and Nights

Here's a Tip: At some theaters you can buy a book of movie tickets. You'll save money on the prices—and the book makes a great present!

Some businesses have times that are *slow*. This means that business is not as good as usual during that time. So the owner lowers prices to get more people to come during that slow time.

This sometimes happens at places like miniature golf courses, swimming pools, the movies, or amusement parks. You can often save money by going out when things aren't crowded.

Look at the prices at Theater on the Square.

Wordwise: A *senior* is an older person, usually at least 65 years of age.

Theater on the Square

Adults	$5.50
Seniors	$3.50
Children under 12	$2.25
Monday nights—all seats	$1.75

You want to save money. What's the best night of the week to go to the movies at this theater?

Calculator Practice

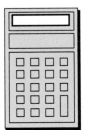

How much would it cost for 6 adults, 5 seniors, and 7 children to go to a movie on Friday?

Step 1:

Enter 6

Press x

Enter 5.50

Press =

Your answer should be: $33

(continued on next page)

Calculator Practice (continued)

Step 2:	Step 3:
Enter 5	Enter 7
Press x	Press x
Enter 3.50	Enter 2.25
Press =	Press =
Your answer should be: $17.5 or $17.50	Your answer should be: $15.75

Step 4:

Enter the answer to Step 1.

Press +

Enter the answer to Step 2.

Press +

Enter the answer to Step 3.

Press =

Your answer should be: $66.25

Here are some recreation costs. Read about each person below. How much would each person spend?

surfboard	$152.50	judo lessons (13)	$100.00
wetsuit	160.00	tennis lessons (8)	90.00
running shoes	55.00	tennis racket	80.00
working out at gym	4.00 a day	tennis balls	2.95 a can

Progress Check 4

Write your answers on a separate sheet of paper.

1. Mia is a runner. She competes in community marathons. She uses 3 pairs of running shoes a year and enters 3 marathons. The fees for the

<table>
<tr><td>

Basics Practice

a.
$90.00
80.00
+ 8.85

b.
152.50
+ 160.00

c. $4.00 x 16 = ?

</td></tr>
</table>

2. Woody is starting to play tennis at the free city
   courts. He buys a racket and 2 cans of tennis balls.
   How much does he spend? If he takes 8 lessons,
   how much will he pay altogether?

3. Troy works out at a gym 3 days a week. How much
   should he budget for the gym every 4 weeks?

4. Chris took 13 judo lessons in the fall and 13 in the
   spring. How much did she spend on training?

5. Lori wants to buy a surfboard and a wetsuit with
   the money she earns at Lido's Fish Restaurant. She
   earns $4.50 an hour, and she works 25 hours a
   week. She makes $200 a week in tips. How long
   will she need to work to pay for the surfing gear?

Comparing Prices to Get the Best Deals

Suppose that your neighbor Lydia wants to take an
aerobics class. Three places in your town are offering
aerobics. They are the Hollyoak Hospital Education
Center, the Parks and Recreation Department, and
Sylvia and Sam's Health Club.

Here are the notices for each class. Read and
compare them.

Hollyoak Hospital Education Center	Parks and Recreation Department	Sylvia and Sam's Health Club
Aerobics for Fitness	Aerobics II	Aerobic Action
Tuesday/Thursday	Monday/Wednesday	Wednesday/Friday
14 meetings	7 weeks, twice weekly	6 weeks/12 meetings
May 13 to June 26	May 1 to June 12	May 17 to June 21
10:00 – 11:00 A.M.	4:15 – 5:30 P.M.	10:30 – 11:30 A.M.
$105.00	$4.50 a class	$90.00

Progress Check 5

Write your answers on a separate piece of paper.

1. How many times a week does Aerobics for Fitness meet? How many weeks will the class last?
2. Are all three of the programs for the same number of weeks? Which one is the shortest?
3. How much will it cost Lydia to take Aerobics for Fitness? How many meetings are there? What would be the cost per meeting?
4. How much does it cost per meeting to take Aerobics II at the Parks and Recreation Department? How many times a week does it meet? How many weeks does it run? How much would it cost if Lydia went to every meeting?
5. How much will Lydia pay for 12 Aerobic Action meetings? What would be the cost of one meeting?
6. Which of these aerobics programs is the least expensive? How much less is Aerobics II than Aerobic Action?
7. Suppose Lydia finds out that she can't go on Monday and Wednesday. She decides to go to Aerobics for Fitness. She needs to buy one pair of leotards at $13.98. She also needs two pairs of tights at $7.95 each. She buys the clothing and pays for the program all on the same day. How much does she spend?
8. Suppose Lydia goes back to Aerobics II for 3 sessions. How much will she spend for these sessions?

Taking Inventory: Budgeting for What You'll Need

Suppose you take **inventory** of your equipment for recreation. You make a list of what you have and what you need. Sometimes your recreation involves getting lots of things together. You might need tools, equipment, and clothes.

Imagine that you're planning your first fishing trip. You will go to Lake Ketchum with a friend. You discuss the trip. Then you list the things you'll need. Here is the list. Next to each item is the price of the item at Jay Estey's Sport Shop.

Jay Estey's Sport Shop

A		B		C	
fishing rod and reel	$35.99	lures (pkg.)	$1.59	hooks (pkg.)	$.69
waders	39.99	fly lures (pkg.)	1.89	floats (med.)	.34
vest	24.99	extra line	1.39	floats (small)	.29
hat	2.00	swivels (pkg.)	1.49	sinkers (pkg.)	.69
tackle box	12.99				

Progress Check 6

Write your answers on a separate piece of paper.

1. You'll want to buy all the items in column A. What will be their total cost?

2. In column B, you'll buy 4 packages of lures at $1.59 each. You'll also buy 1 package of fly lures, the extra line, and 1 package of the swivels. How much will these items cost?

3. In column C, you'll buy 4 packages of hooks. You'll also buy 5 medium floats, 5 small floats, and 1 package of sinkers. How much will those items cost?

4. Add the costs for fishing gear from your answers to 1, 2, and 3. What is the total?

5. You and your friend rent a boat for $15 a day for 3 days. You spend $47.89 on groceries for 3 days. You split the cost of the boat rental and food. What will your share be?

6. The next time you go fishing, you'll have the basic gear. You'll only need to plan for your share of the boat rental, food, and the items in columns B and C. What do you estimate your fishing trip will cost?

7. You're planning 2 fishing trips a year at the same cost as described in question 6. What will you need to budget for the year for fishing?

8. You'll pay half of the $35 cost of gasoline for each trip. What will your total gasoline costs be for 2 trips?

Check Your Budgeting Skills

Below is a list showing the recreational activities eight different people enjoy. The cost of each activity is shown in the third column. The number of times each person likes to do the activity is shown under *How Often*. Use the information to decide how each person should budget for the activity.

Name	Recreation	Cost		How Often?
1. Miguel	listen to live jazz	$6.50		once every 2 weeks
2. Ronnie	horseback riding	15.00	a day	once a week
3. Larry	video games	.25	a game	20 games; twice a week
4. Darnell	amusement park	25.00	book of tickets	once every 2 weeks
5. Corinne	roller skating	4.50		once a week
6. Luis	concerts	15.00	a ticket	once every 2 weeks
7. Susan	movies	5.00	a ticket	once a week
8. Nick	mountain climbing	55.00	per climb	once every 13 weeks

Progress Check 7

Write your answers on a separate piece of paper.

1. Number your paper from 1 to 8. Write the name of each person next to the number. For each person, find the recreation expense for the next 26 weeks. Write that figure beside the person's name.

2. Write the numbers 9 and 10. Next to 9, name the person who will spend the least on recreation in 26 weeks. Next to 10, name the person who will spend the most on recreation.

Math on the Job

1. Abel Morris works at Ketchum Lake. He rents rowboats for $15 a day. Today 20 customers have rented boats. How much will Abel report for the day's total rentals?

2. Sean O'Meara is a fishing guide. He charges customers $90 a day. This week Sean has 5 customers. How much will he earn?

3. Pauline Montana is a buyer for Jay's sporting goods stores. This month, one store sold 30 tennis rackets, another sold 23, and another sold 15. How many rackets will Pauline order to replace those sold?

4. Albert Kurobashi teaches judo classes. He charges $15 per student per lesson. He offers 2 classes a week. Albert has 8 students. How much money will Albert make in 6 weeks?

5. Melinda Cosby manages a motel in a vacation area. The motel owner wants to know the average gross income for each week. Melinda reports to the owner every 4 weeks. In the past 4 weeks, the motel took in $14,700. What is the weekly average?

Chapter Review

Chapter Summary

- Planning for recreation costs can increase your enjoyment of your spare-time activities.

- To figure your costs, you can ask yourself three questions: How much does the activity cost? What are the costs of equipment or clothes? What else might I pay for while I'm doing the activity?

- Estimating costs helps you know how much to budget.

- Sometimes *when* you do something will make a difference as to how much it costs.

- When estimating the cost of lessons, you'll usually figure for a number of weeks.

- Spectator sports can have hidden costs such as programs or parking fees.

- Some sports or recreational activities are much more expensive than others.

- Comparing the cost of the same activity in different places may help you save money.

- Taking an inventory of things you need lets you plan for their cost.

- To accurately estimate costs of recreation, you need to know two things: how much the activity costs, and how often you will be doing the activity.

Chapter Quiz

Write your answers on a separate sheet of paper.

1. Randy takes Tai Chi lessons at $12.50 per lesson, once a week. Karen takes self-defense lessons for $8 twice a week. Who spends more?

2. Tina wants to take hang-gliding lessons. She is told that 8% of hang-gliding students are women. What percentage are men?

3. Name two different things you could spend money for when you go ice-skating at a skating rink.

4. What costs should you consider when planning to go to a spectator sport?
   a. parking and/or transportation
   b. your uniform
   c. refreshments and program

5. You want to take a class. You know it's offered in more than one place. What should you do first to save on cost?
   a. buy gear
   b. rent equipment
   c. compare prices of the classes
   d. sign up

6. Which individual below spends the most in four weeks?

Name	Recreation	Cost	How Often?
a. J. C.	trumpet lessons	$12.50	once a week
b. Ashley	ballet lessons	15.00	2 times a week
c. Hal	concerts	18.00	once every 2 weeks
d. Brenda	dinners out	16.00	once a week

Challenge

Figure the costs of recreational activities that you like to do the most. Decide how many times a month you participate in these activities. How much should you set aside monthly to pay for these activities? How much should you budget for the entire year?

18 Planning a Trip

Carefully planning a trip takes some time but saves you money in the long run.

Chapter Learning Objectives

- List the benefits of joining an automobile association.
- Calculate trip mileage and driving time.
- Figure gas mileage.
- Figure lodging, food, and gas costs.
- Compare costs of travel by car with travel by airplane, train, and bus.
- Review basic math skills in the Appendix at the back of this textbook.

Words to Know

accommodation   a room or lodging

benefit   anything that is for the good of a person or thing

flare   an emergency device that burns with a bright flame to warn of danger

intersection   a crossroad; the place where two roads meet

lodging   a place where you can stay for a time, such as a hotel or a motel

mph   abbreviation for *miles per hour*

route   a course traveled to reach a destination

suburb   a small city, town, village, or district just outside or near a big city

What Do You Take on a Long Car Trip?

If you are going to take a long trip, you need to figure out some things first. Here are some questions you'll need to answer:

1. How many miles will you be traveling?
2. How long will the trip take?
3. How much will gas, food, and **lodging** cost?

The first thing you need is a road map. Some bookstores, variety stores, and gas stations sell road maps.

What About Trip Mileage and Trip Time?

Most road maps have charts or diagrams showing miles between cities. Knowing the mileage of your trip is important.

If you know the mileage, you'll be able to figure how long your trip will take.

Calculating trip mileage is simple if you are going from one big city to another. Do you want to know how long it takes to get from Dallas to Denver? From Helena to Houston? Just use a distance chart, like the one on the next page. Here is how you use it: Look at the left side. Find the name of a city on your **route**. Then look at the headings at the top of the columns. Find another city on your route in the listings at the top. Put your left finger under the city on the left. Put your right finger under the city at the top. Run your fingers along to where the line and the column meet. The number in the box shows the distance between the two cities you chose.

Progress Check 1

Write your answers on a separate piece of paper.

1. How many miles is it from Salt Lake City to San Francisco?

2. How many miles is it from Chicago to Seattle?

3. How many miles would you travel from Houston to Los Angeles?

4. How many miles would you travel from Boise to St. Louis?

5. Imagine you're taking this trip. Find out the total number of miles you would drive:
   a. from Houston to San Francisco.
   b. from San Francisco to Denver.
   c. from Denver to Dallas.
   d. from Dallas back to Houston.

6. How many total miles would you drive on the trip?

Central and Western United States Mileage Chart

	Chicago	Dallas	Denver	Houston	Kansas City	Los Angeles	Milwaukee	Minneapolis–St. Paul	St. Louis	Salt Lake City	San Francisco	Seattle
Albuquerque	1289	639	419	829	787	797	1341	1206	1040	614	1125	1482
Boise	1731	1607	842	1797	1410	856	1721	1443	1660	358	650	505
Cheyenne	965	871	102	1113	648	1163	988	794	898	462	1212	1267
Chicago		936	1012	1085	499	2090	89	399	288	1427	2177	2052
Dallas	936		784	245	499	1398	1009	956	645	1241	1764	2112
Denver	1012	784		1026	616	1128	1035	841	856	495	1245	1347
Des Moines	330	704	679	947	201	1795	358	253	336	1094	1844	1773
El Paso	1434	622	654	755	935	793	1486	1339	1178	869	1197	1740
Grand Canyon N.P.	1691	1041	722	1231	1192	503	1743	1569	1442	383	827	1254
Helena	1441	1576	792	1818	1261	1228	1363	1027	1498	500	1126	611
Houston	1085	245	1026		742	1548	1158	1199	794	1431	1952	2302
Kansas City	499	499	616	742		1591	554	454	253	1110	1860	1872
Lincoln	526	630	486	874	216	1613	551	385	465	912	1662	1672
Little Rock	644	331	957	441	396	1701	717	825	353	1456	2025	2277
Los Angeles	2090	1398	1128	1548	1591		2142	1940	1841	720	401	1144
Memphis	537	464	1035	561	459	1831	619	846	288	1534	2155	2331
Milwaukee	89	1009	1035	1158	554	2142		324	364	1450	2200	1974
Minneapolis–St. Paul	399	956	841	1199	454	1940	324		552	1239	1989	1638
New Orleans	927	498	1282	362	821	1896	1008	1240	685	1739	2262	2610
Oklahoma City	794	210	615	455	347	1352	868	804	504	1108	1676	1962
Omaha	472	656	547	899	202	1656	497	359	454	955	1705	1667
Phoenix	1725	1005	818	1155	1226	390	1777	1636	1476	669	797	1451
Portland	2123	2043	1278	2233	1846	969	2045	1709	2096	789	639	175
St. Louis	288	645	856	794	253	1841	364	552		1360	2110	2109
Salt Lake City	1427	1241	495	1431	1110	720	1450	1239	1360		751	857
San Francisco	2177	1764	1245	1952	1860	401	2200	1989	2110	751		814
Santa Fe	1253	630	360	820	754	863	1300	1142	1006	611	1187	1482
Seattle	2052	2112	1347	2302	1872	1144	1974	1638	2109	857	814	
Spokane	1763	1896	1112	2138	1583	1220	1685	1349	1820	732	909	277
Tulsa	690	265	684	510	244	1448	766	698	402	1177	1772	2031
Wichita	697	367	526	612	195	1397	749	634	448	1005	1721	1852

7. Which trip is longest?

    a. Spokane to St. Louis

    b. Omaha to Seattle

    c. Portland to Chicago

    d. Tulsa to Los Angeles

8. You're driving from Kansas City to Los Angeles. Then you're going to Seattle and back home. How many miles will you travel?

Mileage to small cities and towns can also be found on a road map. Numbers of miles are written beside each stretch of highway. In the example below, miles are listed for the distances between **intersections**.

Box A   Box B

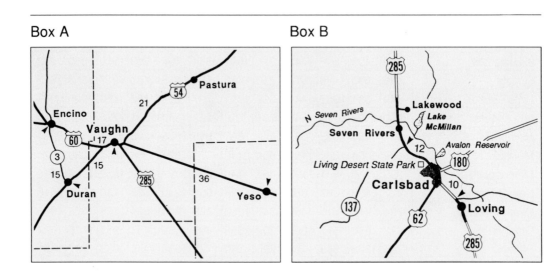

Solve It

Look at Box A. The distance from Encino to Vaughn on Route 60 is 17 miles. How far is it from Vaughn to Yeso on the same route?

If you know your trip mileage, you can figure your driving time. On interstate highways, you can average 55 miles per hour, or 1.1 minutes per mile. On smaller highways, the average is 40 **mph**, or 1.5 minutes per mile. In suburbs and cities, it's 20 mph, or 3 minutes per mile.

Solve It

In Box B at left, it's 12 miles from Seven Rivers into the center of Carlsbad. About 9 of the 12 miles are on a small highway. About 3 of the 12 miles are through **suburbs** and the city. What will the driving time probably be?

Highway driving time 9 x 1.5 = _____ minutes

Suburb/city driving time 3 x 3 = _____ minutes

Highway + suburb/city driving = _____ minutes

Wordwise: *Tourism* is the business of providing transportation, lodging, and food for tourists. In our country, $65 billion a year is spent on tourism.

To figure total trip time, you must add driving time to the time you take for eating, sleeping, and visiting. It's a good idea to take one rest break for every two hours of driving. And after driving four hours or more, you'll probably want to stop to eat.

Progress Check 2

Write your answers on a separate piece of paper.

1. You're going to drive 220 miles on interstate highways, 160 miles on smaller roads, and 20 miles through suburbs. What will your total hours of driving time be?

Calculator Practice

Interstate	Smaller Roads
Step 1	Step 2
Enter 220	Enter 160
Press ÷	Press ÷
Enter 55	Enter 40
Press =	Press =

City/Suburb	Total hours
Step 3	Step 4
Enter 20	Enter Step 1 Answer
Press ÷	Press +
Enter 20	Enter Step 2 Answer
Press =	Press +
	Enter Step 3 Answer
	Press =
	Your answer
	should be: 9

Basics Practice

a.   1,210 ÷ 55 =

b.   2,320 x 55 =

c.   280 ÷ 55 =

2. You'll be driving 1,100 miles on interstate highways. You can drive only 10 hours a day. How many days will it take?

3. You drive eight hours a day for two days. You stop every two hours to rest and every four hours to eat. How many rest breaks will you take? How many meals will you eat?

Adding Hours and Minutes

To add hours and minutes, use a colon between the hours and the minutes, like this:

1:30 (1 hour and 30 minutes).

Remember that each hour has 60 minutes. When minutes total more than 60, add another hour to the left of the colon. The remainder of minutes stays to the right. For example, the driving time from Los Vegas to Ely, Nevada, is 5:45 (five hours and 45 minutes). From Ely to Reno, it's 6:47 (six hours and 47 minutes). What is the total driving time from Las Vegas to Reno? This is how you must figure:

$$
\begin{array}{r}
5:45 \\
+\ 6:47 \\
\hline
11:92 \ = 12:32
\end{array}
$$

Progress Check 3

Write your answers on a separate sheet of paper.

1. On day one, you drive 8 hours and 40 minutes. The next day, you drive 6 hours and 50 minutes. On the third day, you reach your destination. This day, you only drive 3 hours and 10 minutes. How many hours and minutes did you drive in all?

2. It takes 2 hours and 15 minutes to drive from your home to your sister's place. You visit with your sister for 3 hours and 45 minutes. Then you drive back home. How many hours did you spend driving and visiting your sister?

Basics Practice

a.
      138
       46
+ 920

b.
    4:42
+ 5:34

c.
    5:33
− 1:16

What About Food and Lodging?

Did You Know?
You can save money on a trip by camping out. Many bookstores and outdoor stores have lists of campgrounds along highways.

Unless you bring your own food, you'll eat in restaurants on your trip. And unless you camp out, you'll sleep in motels. You need to figure how much money you'll spend for food and lodging.

There are inexpensive restaurants along most highways. Usually you can get breakfast for about $4, lunch for $6, and dinner for $8 or less. How much should you plan to spend on food in a day?

Solve It

$4	breakfast
6	lunch
+ 8	dinner
$?	total daily cost of food

There are inexpensive motels, too, often located near the less expensive restaurants. Usually you can get a motel room for $35 or less. Suppose you'll be on the road for two and a half days (2.5 days). How much will your food and lodging cost?

Solve It

Cost of motels (2 x $35) $ _____

Cost of meals (2.5 x $18) $ _____

Total cost of food and lodging = $ _____

How Do You Figure Gas Mileage?

Here's a Tip: Check your gas mileage regularly. If your car starts getting fewer miles per gallon, something may be wrong. Or it may be time to get your car tuned.

Figuring your car's gas mileage lets you calculate gasoline costs for a trip.

To figure gas mileage, first get a tankful of gas. Set your trip odometer to zero, or write down the miles that appear on the main odometer. When you've used half a tank or more of gas, fill the tank again. Write down the number of miles the odometer has added. Divide that total by the number of gallons of gas you've bought. The answer is the miles your car goes per gallon of gas.

Solve It

Suppose you've driven 315 miles and it takes nine gallons to fill your tank. How many miles per gallon is your car getting?

315 miles ÷ 9 gallons = _____

To figure gasoline costs for your trip, first divide trip mileage by gas mileage. Then multiply the answer by the price per gallon of gas.

Progress Check 4

Write your answers on a separate piece of paper.

1. Gil is going on an 800-mile trip. His gas mileage is 32 miles per gallon. Gas costs $1.12 per gallon. How much will Gil pay for gas?
2. Gil will also pay $70 for motels and $45 for food. With gas, what will be his total cost?

What Can an Automobile Association Do for You?

Automobile associations provide helpful services to car owners. By looking in the phone book, you can find an automobile association in your area. To become a member, you pay a fee that ranges from $30 to $45 a year. Here are some of the **benefits** you will receive as a member:

- Your towing costs will be paid if your car breaks down on the road.
- You'll get free maps and advice on the best routes for your trip.

- You'll get a book that lists motels and descriptions of their **accommodations**. The book will also list restaurants and give prices for both lodging and dining.
- You may receive some special insurance coverage.
- You may receive emergency signs to use if you break down on the road.

Are you planning to take a few trips? Then you might decide that joining an automobile association is a good idea. For example, suppose your car breaks down. Getting towed ten miles to the garage will cost at least $50. It would be free if you were an automobile association member. How much would you save?

Solve It

$50   cost of getting towed
– $35   sample auto association membership fee
?   amount saved if you were towed just once

How Can You Prepare for an Emergency?

Every car should carry **flares** or a flashing lantern in case of an emergency. At your local auto parts store, flares will cost about $1.75 each. A flashing lantern that uses energy from your car battery costs about $10.99. You need at least 4 flares. What is the difference in cost?

Solve It

Cost of a flashing lantern $10.99
Cost of 4 flares (4 x $1.75) $ _____
How much more or less do flares cost? $ _____

What Other Safety Steps Should You Take?

Here's a Tip: To check for worn tires, put a Lincoln penny, head first, into a groove in the tread. If the top of Lincoln's head disappears, the tire is still good. If not, you need a new tire.

Before leaving, you need to have a mechanic check your engine belts. It's also important to have your brake fluid and your radiator fluid levels checked. And your tires should be checked to see if they have enough tread.

Has it been quite a while since your car had an oil change? If so, you may need to get your oil and oil filter changed before you go. During the trip, check the oil frequently. Not having enough oil can burn up your engine.

Check your car's tire pressure, too. It should be near to the maximum printed on the tire sidewall. Tires too soft or too hard can blow out.

Progress Check 5

Write your answer on a separate sheet of paper.

You buy 5 flares at $1.75 each and a flashlight for $4.69. How much does your safety equipment cost?

Is It Less Expensive to Go by Car?

You're going from Chicago to Denver. You wonder if driving your car is less expensive than other transportation. The road distance is 1,012 miles. By car, the trip will take 2 days. Your costs for food, lodging, and gas will be $107.

You call an airline. A one-way ticket costs $204. You call the train company. Train fare is $142, and you'll spend $16 on meals. You call a bus line.

Bus fare is $94. But the bus takes longer than the train, so you'll need $24 for meals. What is the total cost of each of these kinds of transportation?

Solve It

	Airplane	Train	Bus
Ticket cost	$204	$142	$94
Food cost	$ —	$16	$24
Total cost	$ —	$ —	$ —

Progress Check 6

Write your answers on a separate piece of paper.

1. Which is the least expensive way to travel from Chicago to Denver? Which is the most expensive? How much less is the lowest cost than the highest cost?

2. Bargain round-trip bus fare is $159, and meals are $48. Would this be less expensive than a round trip by car? How much more or less?

Math on the Job

1. Marcie Schulman is a drama teacher. She is taking 22 students to a play in another city. The group will get tickets, lodging, and dinner for $275. The cost will be divided evenly among the students. How much will Marcie tell each student to pay?

2. Jo Leonard is the manager at the Inn by the Sea. The rates are $65 for one person, $75 for two people, and $10 for a rollaway bed. Jo will increase all rates by 10% on the first of the month. How much will each new rate be?

3. Kevin Moran is a travel agent. His customer has asked for the least expensive flight on any airline from San Jose, California, to Seattle, Washington. Tim finds the lowest cost on StayAflight Airlines. It is $198. The reservation is made 14 days in advance. Otherwise, the flight costs $253. What is the difference between the two prices Tim will offer his customer?

4. Alfredo Osorio leads backpacking trips. He is taking a group on a trip from Seagull Point to Swift River. Alfredo needs to figure the distance of the hike. The distance from Seagull Point to Great Vista is 6.5 miles. The distance from Great Vista to Soto Creek is 3.2 miles. The distance from Soto Creek to Swift River is 4.7 miles. How many miles will the group hike to Swift River and back again?

5. Kara McCullough works at an automobile association. Kara collects state tax for the sales of cars between two private parties. An association member has bought a used car for $2,800. The sales tax in Kara's state is 6%. How much will she collect from the new owner of the car?

6. Alex and Melissa are planning a trip from Chicago, Illinois to Orlando, Florida. Round trip air fare will cost $235 per person. If they take a train, the round trip fare is $250 per person and the second person receives a 10 percent discount. Which form of travel, airplane or train, would cost the least?

Chapter Review

Chapter Summary

- When you take a long trip, you need to know three things: how many miles you'll drive, how long the trip will take, and what it will cost for gas, food, and lodging.

- If you know the mileage of your trip, you can figure out how long it will take.

- Many road maps have charts or diagrams that can help you figure mileage.

- Some maps help you figure how much time your trip will take.

- To estimate your food expense, figure the total cost per day for meals. Then multiply the total cost by the number of days.

- You would estimate the costs of your lodging by using a certain price per day.

- To estimate the gas cost for the trip, you'll need to figure your gas mileage.

- An automobile association can provide helpful services that will make your traveling easier and safer.

- When you plan a trip, you may want to compare costs of driving to costs of flying or taking the train or bus.

Chapter Quiz

Write your answers on a separate sheet of paper.

1. Before you go on a trip, you need to know how many miles you'll be driving. What are two other things you need to know so you can figure cost?

2. How can you find out exactly how many miles it is from one city to another?

3. You're going to drive 165 miles on interstate highways, 160 on smaller roads, and 20 miles through suburbs. The speed limit on interstate highways is 55 mph. On smaller highways, it's 40 mph. In suburbs and cities, it's 20 mph. What will be your total hours of driving time?

4. You compare costs of a trip from San Francisco, California, to Washington, D.C. By plane it's $360. By bus it's $198. If you take the bus, you'll spend about $60 for food. What will be the cost difference between the bus trip and the plane trip?

5. You plan to spend $30 a night for lodging. You will be on the road for 3 nights. How much should you estimate for lodging costs?

6. You have driven 286 miles, and it takes 11 gallons to fill your tank. How many miles per gallon is your car getting?

7. You are planning a trip from Santa Fe, New Mexico, to El Paso, Texas. It takes about 1:08 to drive from Santa Fe to Albuquerque. It takes 4:16 from Albuquerque to Las Cruces. It takes 0:52 from Las Cruces to El Paso. What is the total driving time?

Challenge

Think about a place you've always wanted to go. What place is it? What state is it in? Get a road map that has a section showing routes from the area where you live to the state you're traveling to. Write down the number of miles it will take to get there. Give yourself 32 miles per gallon for gas mileage. Find out the price of regular unleaded gas. Figure your gasoline cost for the trip. Will you be away overnight? If so, figure $35 per night for lodging. Figure $4 for each breakfast, $6 for lunch, and $8 for dinner. What will be your total trip cost?

Unit Nine Review

Read the questions. On a separate piece of paper answer *Yes* or *No*. Then tell why or why not.

1. Do time and day affect the cost of a recreational activity?

2. Suppose Juan wants to take an inventory of his sports equipment. He makes a list of the things he wants to buy. Is that all he has to do?

3. Susan plans to bowl every Thursday. She writes down the cost of the games she'll play. Is she budgeting for all her bowling expenses?

4. Is it true that all sports cost about the same to play?

5. Myung says that to estimate the cost of recreation, you need to know these things: how much the activity costs and how often you want to do it. Is she right?

6. Would a road atlas be helpful if you were driving from Dallas to Denver? Why or why not?

7. If you know your trip mileage, can you figure out your driving time?

8. Brenda is driving from Columbia, Missouri, to Baltimore, Maryland. The distance is exactly 1,000 miles. If she drives at 55 miles an hour for 8 hours a day, can she make the trip in 2 days?

9. Brenda filled her tank with gas when she left Columbia. Her tank holds 12 gallons. If Brenda's car gets 24 miles a gallon, will she have to stop for gas before she gets to Baltimore? (Hint: multiply the number of miles to the gallon by 12 first.)

10. Are there any cost-saving benefits of joining an automobile association?

Glossary

abbreviated   made shorter

accommodation   a room or lodging

ad   a short form of the word *advertisement*

allowance   a reduction in your tax for each person you support, including yourself

annual percentage rate   the amount (in percent) of the finance charge

appearance   the way something looks

appliance   a tool or machine for doing a task, like a vacuum cleaner, washing machine, or can opener

application   form used to ask for something

asterisk   a star-shaped symbol (*) used to refer to a special note on a printed page

ATM   Automated Teller Machine, a walk-up computer station on the outside of the bank; machine used by a bank customer to make deposits and withdrawals

authorized   approved; official; correct

balance   the money left in a bank account

balance of the loan   the amount left to pay

balanced budget   a situation in which the total outgo matches income

bank account   bank record of the money a customer deposits and withdraws

bank statement   a bank form that is sent each month to the customer; a form listing all the checks paid, deposits made, ATM uses, service charges, and the account's balance

benefit   anything that is for the good of a person or thing

Blue Book   a book that shows the wholesale and retail prices of cars

budget   a plan for spending and saving money

budget item   a line with details about a particular expense or savings entry

calorie   unit of energy supplied by food

cancelled check   any check the bank pays and subtracts from your checking account

car insurance   protection you buy against the cost of car accidents and theft

catalog   a listing of products you can order and have sent to you

check register   a small booklet to use to keep track of your balance when you write checks or make a deposit or a withdrawl

cholesterol   a waxy substance in animal fats

clearance sale   an event in which many items are marked down for quick sale

co-applicant   a person who applies with another person for a service or privilege

collateral   something used as security for a loan

collision   insurance that pays for the repair of your car after an accident

compound interest   interest on the principal (money in a savings account) and on the interest already earned

comprehensive   insurance that covers damage from such things as fire and flood

cosigner someone who signs a loan contract with a borrower and promises to pay if the borrower doesn't pay

coverage protection against the costs of accidents, theft, or other risks

credit application a form you fill out to get credit so you can buy something now but pay for it later

credit card a card that allows you to buy things without using cash

credit references people or businesses that can show that you pay your bills and loan payments regularly

currency folding money; money in bills, such as a dollar bill or a five-dollar bill

dealer a business person who sells cars or other items

debt money that is owed

deductible the amount of money you pay for repairs or injuries before the insurance company pays

deduction an amount subtracted from gross pay for a tax, a benefit, a service, or a membership

deposit money a renter may have to pay before moving in; money that will be returned when the renter moves out if the place is clean and has not been damaged; to put money into a bank account; money put into a bank account

deposit slip a slip of paper kept by the bank to show how much money you put into your account

diet the food and drink that is consumed by a person

discount the amount taken off a regular price

dividend money earned as profit by a company and divided among people who invested money in the company

down payment money paid toward the total price of an item

earnings statement the check stub attached to your paycheck listing gross pay, deductions, and net pay

employee a person who works for another person or business for pay

employment work; what a person does to earn a living

employment agency a company that, for a fee, helps people find jobs

endorse to sign your name on the back of a check

entry something entered into a book or booklet

estimate a judgment of about how many or about how much

expenses money spent on various things that are needed or wanted; costs

factory outlet a self-service, low-priced store that sells items directly from the factory where they were made

finance charge a fee for borrowing money

fixed unchanging; remaining the same

fixed interest rate a percentage that doesn't change

flare an emergency device that burns with a bright flame to warn of danger

furnishings furniture, appliances, rugs, curtains, and other items used in a home

generic without a brand name; not advertised and not colorfully packaged

gram   a unit of weight in the metric system; about twenty-eight grams equal one ounce

gross pay   amount of salary earned

hourly   every 60 minutes

income   money received for working, or from investments or other sources

ingredient   one of the parts of a mixture

insurance   protection against losses or damage

interest   the amount it costs to use money that is lent

intersection   a crossroad; the place where two roads meet

inventory   a list of supplies, equipment, or merchandise

layaway plan   a plan in which something is marked sold but is kept in the store until you finish paying for it

lb.   abbreviation for pound; unit of weight

lease   a written agreement between a renter and the owner of the place being rented

liability   insurance that pays for other people's injuries and property damage if you caused the accident

lien   a claim on property or possessions for payment of a debt

loan   money that is borrowed

lodging   a place where one can stay for a time, such as a hotel or a motel

markup   the difference between the wholesale, or store's, price and the price the store charges the customer

maximum   the greatest possible amount

merchandise   goods for sale; articles bought and sold

mileage   the total miles a car has been driven; also the average number of miles a car will go on a gallon of gas

minimum   the least possible amount

monthly   each month

monthly service charge   a bank's fee for taking care of an account

mph   abbreviation for *miles per hour*

net pay   amount of salary received after deductions have been taken

nutritional value   the amount of the proteins, vitamins, and minerals that contribute to good health

nutritious   nourishing; valuable as food

outgo   money paid out for expenses

overtime   beyond regular hours

oz.   abbreviation for ounce; unit of weight

per   for each

pkg.   abbreviation for *package*

predict   to make a guess about the future

premium   money paid to a company for insurance

prescription   a doctor's direction or order for preparing and using medicine

principal   money in a savings account or owed on a bill, not counting interest

priority   coming before something else in order of importance

produce   vegetables and fruit

promissory note   a written promise to pay back a loan or money you owe

protein a substance that is a necessary part of the cells of animals and plants

qualify to show you're able to take on a responsibility, job, or task

quality how good something is

refund money returned from a deposit or other money paid out

rental application an information form filled out by someone who wants to rent property

retail the price stores charge the customer

route a course traveled to reach a destination

salary fixed pay for regular work

saturated fat lard, suet, butterfat, chicken fat, and others that stay solid at room temperature

signature card a card with the name, address, and authorized signature of a bank customer

simple interest interest on the principal only

spectator sport a sport, or athletic event, that has spectators, or people, who watch but don't take part

storewide throughout the whole store

suburb a small city, town, village, or district just outside or near a big city

tax money paid to the national treasury or the state treasury

teller a person who works in a bank helping customers with deposits, withdrawals, and check-cashing

time card a paper or card on which hours worked by an employee are recorded

time payments money paid, usually monthly, until the total bill is paid

transfer to move money from one budget line to another

uninsured motorist coverage insurance that pays for some of your costs if an uninsured driver hits your car

unpaid balance amount of money left to pay toward the total price

unsaturated fat oils like olive oil, corn oil, safflower oil, and others that are liquid at room temperature

utilities services such as electricity, gas, water, and garbage pickup

variable changing from time to time

variable interest rate a percentage that changes or varies

verification proof of the truth

wage amount paid for work

warranty a promise that something a company sells will last a certain time, or else you will get money back

weekly every seven days

wholesale the price a store pays for an item

withdrawal money taken out of a bank account

withheld kept out

Appendix

Appendix A: Deciding How to Solve a Problem

To decide which operation to use, follow these steps:

1. Think about the problem. Write down the information you have available.
2. Decide what information is missing.
3. Formulate a word problem. Are there any clue words in your problem?
4. Think about what a sensible answer might be. Would it be larger or smaller than the largest number in your problem?
5. If your sensible answer is a larger number, you should add or multiply. If your sensible number is a smaller number, you should subtract or divide.

An example of a word problem is: If I have $56.12 in my checking account, how much will I have left after I make out a check for $11.03? "How much will I have left" are your clue words. They tell you to subtract.

Clue in to Clue Words

Certain words and groups of words in a math problem tell you whether to add, subtract, multiply, or divide.

Add when clue words in your problem tell you to put numbers together. Look for words like:

- in all
- together
- all together
- total
- both

Subtract when clue words in your problem tell you to find the difference between numbers. Look for words like:

- how many more
- how many less
- what's the difference
- how much more
- deduct the amount
- how much longer
- how many left

Multiply when clue words in your problem tell you to add a number to itself one or more times. Look for words like:

- in five months
- how many a year
- for six hours at $13
- what's 10% of

Divide when clue words in your problem tell you to separate numbers into groups. Look for words like:

- how much does each
- how many times each
- how much per
- what percentage is one number of another
- into how many
- what's half (a quarter) of the amount

Appendix B: Brush Up on Addition

Key Words

- **add**   to put numbers together to find a total amount
- **addends**   the numbers to be added
- **sum** or **total**   the amount obtained by adding
- **renaming**   to break down a number into its parts
- **equal**   the same as
- **rounding**   changing numbers to make them easier to work with
- **estimate**   to make a guess about the value of something or about the answer to a problem
- **digit**   the symbols used to write numbers: 0, 1, 2, 3, 4, 5, 6, 7, 8, and 9

When you round 23 to the nearest tens number, you change it to 20.

Basic Addition Facts

- **Order**   You can add whole numbers in any order. The sum will not change.

```
   1        3        3
   3        1        4
 + 4      + 4      + 1
 ───      ───      ───
   8        8        8
```

- **Adding Zero**   When 0 is added to a number, the number stays the same.

```
   3       31       310
 + 0      + 0      +  0
 ───      ───      ────
   3       31       310
```

- **Adding Large Numbers**   To add large numbers, start with the digits in the ones place. Then add the digits in the tens place. Work from right to left, adding one place at a time.

```
        add third
        add second
        add first
         │ │ │
         2 3 1
       + 1 3 0
```

- **Renaming**   Sometimes digits in a place add up to 10 or more. In that case, you must rename the sum. Do it this way: First add the digits in the ones place. If the number is 10 or larger, rename it. Add the digit on the right to the ones column. Add the digit on the left to the tens column. Do the same for the other columns, if they add up to 10 or more than 10.

```
              tens ones
              |    |
       48     1
     + 24       4  8
              + 2  4
                7  2
```

- **Estimating**   Estimating gives you a quick idea of what the number will be. Follow these steps: First round each number. Then add these numbers. The sum is your estimate.

- **Rounding**   To round to the tens place: If the digit in the ones place is 5 or more, add 1 to the digit in the tens place. If the digit in the ones place is less than 5, do not change the digit in the tens place. To round to the hundreds place: If the digit in the tens place is 5 or more, add 1 to the digit in the hundreds place. If the digit in the tens place is less than 5, do not change the digit in the hundreds place. Then change the digit in the tens place to 0.

```
   148    rounds to   150
 + 302    rounds to   300
                       450
    the estimate is ──┘
```

Clue Words

Words and groups of words like these tell you to put numbers together. They tell you to add.

- in all
- together
- all together
- total
- both

Appendix C: Brush Up on Subtraction

Key Words

- **subtract** to take away one number from another; to find the difference between two numbers.
- **difference** the amount by which one number is larger or smaller than another; the amount that remains after one number is subtracted from another.

Basic Subtraction Facts

- **Order** Subtraction with whole numbers can only be done in one order. You must subtract the smaller number from the larger number.

  You can subtract $5 - 3$, but not $3 - 5$.

- **Subtracting Zero** When you subtract 0 from a whole number, the whole number stays the same. When you subtract a number from itself, the answer is zero.

  $9 - 0 = 9$
  $9 - 9 = 0$

- **Subtracting Large Numbers** To subtract large numbers, start with the digits in the ones place. Then go on to the digits in the tens place. Work from right to left, subtracting one place at a time.

- **Renaming**   Sometimes you cannot subtract the digits in a column. In that case, you must rename to find the difference. To do this, you must first rename to show more ones (or tens or hundreds). Then subtract the digits in the ones (or tens or hundreds) place. Finally, subtract the new number of digits in the tens (or hundreds) place.

  a.
  ```
       4 12
       5̷ 2̷
     − 1  7
  ```

  b.
  ```
       4 12
       5̷ 2̷
     − 1  7
            5
  ```

  c.
  ```
       4 12
       5̷ 2̷
     − 1  7
         3  5
  ```

- **Estimating**   Estimating quickly gives you a rough answer. Follow these steps: Round the numbers to the same place. Then subtract the numbers. The difference is your estimate.

  ```
     392   rounds to   400
   − 107   rounds to   100
                        300
        the estimate is ⌐
  ```

- **Checking**   Addition and subtraction are opposite operations. You can check your subtraction by adding.

  446 − 243 = 203

  203 + 243 = 446

Clue Words

Words and groups of words like these tell you to find the difference between numbers. They tell you to subtract.

- how many more
- how many less
- what's the difference
- how much more
- deduct the amount
- how much longer
- how many left

Appendix D: Brush Up on Multiplication

Key Words

- **multiply** to add a number to itself one or more times
- **multiplicand** the first factor
- **multiplier** the second factor
- **product** the answer in a multiplication problem

Basic Multiplication Facts

- **Order** You can multiply factors in any order. The product will not change.

$$\begin{array}{r} 3 \\ \times\ 2 \\ \hline 6 \end{array} \qquad \begin{array}{r} 2 \\ \times\ 3 \\ \hline 6 \end{array}$$

- **Multiplying by Zero or One** When you multiply a whole number by zero, the answer is zero. When you multiply zero by any whole number, the answer is zero. When you multiply any whole number by one, the answer stays the same.

$$3 \times 0 = 0$$
$$0 \times 6 = 0$$
$$6 \times 1 = 6$$

- **Multiplying Large Numbers** To multiply large numbers, start by multiplying the digit in the ones place of the multiplier to the digit in the ones place in the multiplicand. Then multiply the digit in the ones place of the multiplier to the digit in the tens place in the multiplicand. Continue until you have multiplied all the digits in the multiplicand by the digit in the ones place of the multiplier. Follow the same procedure using the digit in the tens place of the multiplier. Remember to add a zero because you are multiplying by tens. If the multiplicand has

$$\begin{array}{r} 2\ 3\ 2 \\ \times\ \ 3\,2 \\ \hline 4\ 6\ 4 \\ 6\ 9\ 6\ \ \\ \hline 7\ 4\ 2\ 4 \end{array}$$ —— product of 232 x 2

$$\begin{array}{r} 2\ 3\ 2 \\ \times\ \ 3\,2 \\ \hline 4\ 6\ 4 \\ 6\ 9\ 6\ 0 \\ \hline 7\ 4\ 2\ 4 \end{array}$$ —— product of 232 x 30

3 or more digits, you repeat the procedure with each digit.

```
   2 3 2
 x   3 2
   4 6 4
 6 9 6 0
 7 4 2 4 —— sum of
              products
```

- **Estimating**   Estimating gives you a quick, close idea of what an answer will be. Follow these steps: Round each factor to the same place. Then multiply the factors. Your product will be the estimate. Remember that, in multiplication, your estimated answer will not be as close to the real answer as it would in addition or subtraction.

- **Checking**   The answer to a multiplication problem can be checked by dividing the product by one of the factors.

$$2,142 \times 2 = 4,286$$

$$4,286 \div 2 = 2,142$$

Clue Words

Words and groups of words like these tell you to put numbers together. They tell you to multiply.

- in five months
- how many a year
- for six hours at $13
- what's 10% of

Appendix E: Brush Up on Division

Key Words

- **divide**   to find out how many times one number contains another; to subtract a number from itself one or more times.
- **dividend**   the number to be divided
- **divisor**   the number to divide by
- **quotient**   the answer in a division problem
- **remainder**   the number left over in a division problem

Basic Division Facts

- **Order**   Division with whole numbers can only be done in one order. The divisor must be smaller than the dividend.
- **Dividing a Number by Itself**   When you divide any number by itself, the answer is 1. When you divide any number by one, the number stays the same.

    $6 \div 6 = 1$

    $6 \div 1 = 6$

- **Dividing Large Numbers**   Follow these steps or use the division chart in the back of this book. First, find out how many times the divisor fits into the first digit to the left of the dividend. (If the first number in the dividend is smaller than the divisor you will also have to use the second and perhaps the third digit of the divisor.) Then multiply your result (the quotient) by the divisor. Subtract this product from the dividend. Bring down the next digit in the dividend. Keep repeating these steps until you complete the answer.

$$
\begin{array}{r}
155 \\
6\overline{)930} \\
6\downarrow \\
\hline
33 \\
30\downarrow \\
\hline
30 \\
30 \\
\hline
0
\end{array}
$$

- **Estimating**   Estimating gives you a quick, close idea of what an answer will be. Follow these steps: Round the divisor and the dividend to the same place. Divide them. Your quotient will be the estimate.

- **Remainder**   Sometimes a number does not divide evenly into another. Then the quotient has a leftover number, or a remainder.

$$\begin{array}{r} 12\,R^1 \\ 2\overline{)25} \\ \end{array} = 12\tfrac{1}{2}$$

$$\begin{array}{r} \underline{2} \\ 05 \\ \underline{04} \\ 1 \end{array}$$

- **Checking**   You can check the answer to a division problem by multiplying the quotient by the divisor.

$$6 \div 3 = 2$$

$$3 \times 2 = 6$$

Clue Words

Words and groups of words like these tell you to separate numbers into groups. They tell you to divide.

- how much does each
- how many times each
- how much per
- what percentage is one number or another
- into how many
- what's half (a quarter) of the amount

Appendix F: Brush Up on Percents

Key Words

- **percent**   a part of a whole that has been divided into 100 equal parts. (The sign of percent is %.)
- **equivalent**   the same; equal

Basic Percent Facts

- **Working with Percents**   A whole is 100%. Any percent number less than 100% is less than a whole. Any percent number more than 100% is more than a whole.

- **Equivalent Forms**   A number can be expressed as a percent, a decimal, or a fraction and still have the same value. For example, 1/2, .5, and 50% are equivalent forms.

- **Changing Percents**   You can add percents just as you would add whole numbers, but you can't multiply or divide by a percent. So you must first change the percent to an equivalent decimal or fraction.

- **Changing Percents to Decimals**   To change percents to decimals, follow these steps: First take away the % sign. Place a decimal point to the right of the last digit. Then move the decimal point two places to the left.

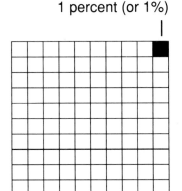

1 percent (or 1%)

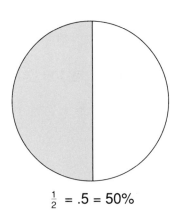

$\frac{1}{2} = .5 = 50\%$

You can't eat 125% of one pie no matter how hungry you are!

15%

.15.

.15

- **Changing Decimals to Percent** To change decimals to percents, follow these steps: First, move the decimal point two places to the right. Then add the percent sign.

$$.16\underset{\smile}{5}$$

16.5%

- **Changing Percents to Fractions** To change percents to fractions, follow these steps: Write the percent as a fraction with the denominator 1. Do not write the % sign. Multiply the fraction by 1/100. Reduce the answer to lowest terms, if necessary. If the percent is a fraction, multiply it by 1/100 directly. If the percent is a mixed number, convert it to an improper fraction before you multiply it by 1/100.

$$6\% = \frac{6}{1} \times \frac{1}{100} = \frac{6}{100}$$

$$\frac{\overset{3}{\cancel{6}}}{\underset{50}{\cancel{100}}} = \frac{3}{50}$$

- **Changing Fractions to Percents** To change a fraction to a percent, follow these steps: Divide the numerator by the denominator. Add a decimal point and two zeros to the dividend. Then find the quotient to two decimal places. Remove the decimal point and write a percent sign.

$$\frac{2}{3} = 3\overline{)2.00}$$

$$\begin{array}{r} .66 \\ 3\overline{)2.00} \\ \underline{18} \\ 20 \\ \underline{18} \\ 2 \end{array} \text{R}^2 = .66\tfrac{2}{3} = 66\tfrac{2}{3}\%$$

- **Changing Mixed Numbers to Percents** To change mixed numbers to a percent, first change the mixed number to an improper fraction. Then follow the steps for changing a fraction to a percent.

$$2\tfrac{1}{2} = \tfrac{5}{2} = 2\overline{)5.00} = 250\%$$

- **Comparing Percents, Decimals, and Fractions** To compare different percents, decimals, and fractions, you must first change them to the same form. In other words, if you are comparing a percent and a fraction, you must first change the percent to an equivalent fraction following the steps given on page 319. If necessary, change the fractions so that they have a common denominator. (See Brush Up on Fractions in Appendix G if you need help.) Then compare numerators.

- **Finding the Percent of a Number**   To find the percent of a number, follow these steps: First, change the percent to a decimal. Then multiply the other number in the problem by the decimal.

32% of 78

$32.\% = .32$

$$
\begin{array}{r}
78 \\
\times\ .32 \\
\hline
156 \\
234 \\
\hline
24.96 = 32\% \text{ of } 78
\end{array}
$$

- **Finding a Number When a Percent Is Known** To find a number when the percent is known, follow these steps: First change the percent to a decimal. Then divide the other number in the problem by the decimal.

20% of _____ = 5

$20.\% = .20$

$$
\begin{array}{r}
25. \\
.20\,\overline{)5.00} \\
\underline{40} \\
100 \\
100 \\
\end{array}
$$

20% of ___25___ = 5

- **Finding What Percent One Number Is of Another**   To find out what percent one number is of another number, follow these steps: First express both numbers as one fraction. The denominator will be the number that represents the whole. The numerator will be the number that represents the percent. Then divide the numerator by the denominator. Add a decimal point and two zeros to the dividend. Then write the quotient as a percent.

There are 50 students in the class. 10 of them are going to Joe's party. What percent of the class is going to Joe's party?

Step 1

$\dfrac{10 \text{ students at party}}{50 \text{ class}}$

Step 2

$$\begin{array}{r} .20 = 20\% \\ 50\overline{)10.00} \\ \underline{10\ 0} \\ 00 \end{array}$$

20% of the class is going to Joe's party

- **Estimating Percents**   To estimate percents, remember: If the percent of the number you are trying to find is less than 100%, your answer will be smaller than the whole. Also, check to see that your answer makes sense. For example, you know that 90% is a very large part of the whole. 90% of a number will be close to that number. 20% of a whole is a small number. Your answer will be much smaller than your original number.

Appendix G: Brush Up on Fractions

Key Words

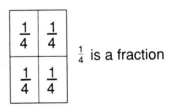

- **fraction**   a number that expresses part of a whole unit; 2/3 is a fraction

- **denominator**   the bottom number in a fraction; the denominator tells how many equal parts there are in the whole unit

- **numerator**   the top number in a fraction; the numerator tells how many parts of the whole unit are being represented

- **lowest terms**   a fraction is in its lowest terms when only 1 divides evenly into both the numerator and the denominator

- **mixed number**   a number made up of a whole number and a fraction

- **like fractions**   fractions with the same denominator

- **unlike fractions**   fractions with different denominators

- **equivalent fractions**   fractions whose numbers are different but whose values are the same

Basic Fraction Facts

- **Adding Like Fractions**   To add like fractions, follow these steps: First, add the numerator. Keep the denominators the same. Then, if necessary, reduce the sum to its lowest terms.

$$\frac{3}{8} + \frac{3}{8} = \frac{\overset{3}{\cancel{6}}}{\underset{4}{\cancel{8}}}$$

$$\frac{3}{8} + \frac{3}{8} = \frac{3}{4}$$

- **Adding Unlike Fractions**   To add unlike fractions, follow these steps: First, change the fractions you want to add to equivalent like fractions. (You can do this by multiplying the denominators.) Add the numerators. Keep the denominators the same. Then, if necessary, reduce the sum to its lowest term.

$$\begin{aligned} \frac{1}{3} &= \frac{4}{12} \\ + \frac{1}{4} &= \frac{3}{12} \\ \hline & \frac{7}{12} \end{aligned}$$

$$\frac{1}{3} + \frac{1}{4} = \frac{7}{12}$$

- **Subtracting Like Fractions**   To subtract like fractions, follow these steps: First, subtract the numerators. Keep the denominators the same. Then, if necessary, reduce the difference to its lowest terms.

$$\frac{5}{8} - \frac{1}{8} = \frac{\overset{1}{\cancel{4}}}{\underset{2}{\cancel{8}}}$$

$$\frac{5}{8} - \frac{1}{8} = \frac{1}{2}$$

- **Subtracting Unlike Fractions**   To subtract unlike fractions, follow these steps: First, change the fractions you want to subtract to like fractions. (You can do this by multiplying the denominators.) Subtract the numerators. Keep the denominators the same. Reduce the difference to the lowest terms.

$$\begin{aligned} \frac{4}{5} &= \frac{8}{10} \\ - \frac{1}{2} &= \frac{5}{10} \\ \hline & \frac{3}{10} \end{aligned}$$

$$\frac{4}{5} - \frac{1}{2} = \frac{3}{10}$$

- **Multiplying Fractions**   To multiply fractions, follow these steps: First, multiply the numerators. Then multiply the denominators. Reduce the product to its lowest terms. Remember: When you are multiplying fractions you don't have to change them to like fractions first.

$$\frac{3}{4} \times \frac{2}{5} = \frac{6}{20}$$

$$\frac{3}{4} \times \frac{2}{5} = \frac{\overset{3}{\cancel{6}}}{\underset{10}{\cancel{20}}}$$

$$\frac{3}{4} \times \frac{2}{5} = \frac{3}{10}$$

- **Dividing Fractions**   To divide fractions, follow these steps: First, invert the second fraction (make the numerator the denominator, and the denominator the numerator). Then change the division sign to a multiplication sign. Cancel, if possible (divide the numerator of one fraction and the denominator of another by the same number). Multiply the numerators. Then, multiply the denominators.

$$\frac{1}{2} \div \frac{3}{4} =$$

Invert

$$\frac{1}{2} \times \frac{4}{3} =$$

cancel and multiply

$$\frac{1}{\cancel{2}} \times \frac{\overset{2}{\cancel{4}}}{3} = \frac{2}{3}$$

$$\frac{1}{2} \div \frac{3}{4} = \frac{2}{3}$$

- **Renaming**   Sometimes you have to rename whole and mixed numbers in order to add, subtract, multiply, or divide fractions. After you complete the operation, you may have to rename again.

$$\blacksquare \ \blacksquare + \blacksquare \ \blacksquare \ \blacksquare =$$

$$1\frac{3}{4} \quad + \quad 2\frac{1}{2} \quad =$$

$$\frac{7}{4} + \frac{5}{2} =$$

$$\frac{7}{4} + \frac{10}{4} = \frac{17}{4} = 4\frac{1}{4}$$

324   Appendix G: Brush Up on Fractions

Appendix H: Brush Up on Decimals

Key Words

- **decimals**   fractions with denominators of 10, 100, 1000, and so on, written with a point followed by digits to the right. (Cents are one example of decimals; twenty-five cents is .25 of a dollar.)
- **decimal point**   the dot written in a decimal
- **mixed decimal**   a number containing a whole number and a decimal. ($12.36 is a mixed decimal.)

$\frac{1}{10} = .1 \qquad \frac{2}{10} = .2$

$\frac{1}{100} = .01 \qquad \frac{2}{100} = .02$

Basic Decimal Facts

- **Zeros in Decimals**   Zeros added after the last digit to the right of the decimal point do not change the decimal. Zeros added between the decimal point and the first digit to the right do change the decimal.

  $.36 = .3600$

  $.36$ does not $= .036$

- **Adding Decimals**   To add decimals, follow these steps: First line up the decimals in your numbers so that the decimal points are directly one under the other. If necessary, write zeros so all the decimals have the same number of places. Then add the decimals just the way you add whole numbers. Put a decimal point in the sum. Place it so that it lines up under the other decimal points.

  ```
    32.85
      .60
    14.00
  + 55.37
   102.82
  ```

- **Subtracting Decimals**   To subtract decimals, follow these steps: First, line up the numbers so the decimal points are one under the other. Then write ending zeros so all the decimals have the same number of places. Subtract the decimals just the way you subtract whole numbers.

  ```
    87.326
  − 43.110
    44.216
  ```

Put a decimal point in the difference. Place it so that it lines up under the other decimal points.

- **Multiplying Decimals**   To multiply decimals, follow these steps: First, line up the numbers so that the decimal points are one under the other. Multiply the decimals just the way you multiply whole numbers. Count the number of decimal places in the numbers you have multiplied. Start at the far right in your answer. Count the same number of decimal places. Put in a decimal point.

$$
\begin{array}{r}
15.34 \\
\times\ 4.2 \\
\hline
3068 \\
61360 \\
\hline
64.428 \\
\end{array}
$$ — 3 decimal places

- **Multiplying Decimals by 10, 100, 1,000**   To multiply decimals by 10, 100, or 1,000, follow these steps: First, count the zeros (for example, 1,000 has 3). Move the decimal point in your other number. Move it to the right one place for each zero. Add more zeros if necessary.

$32.3 \times 10 = 32.3. = 323$

$32.3 \times 100 = 32.30.$
$= 3,230$

$32.3 \times 1,000 = 32.300.$
$= 32,300$

- **Dividing Decimals by Whole Numbers**   To divide decimals by whole numbers, follow these steps: First, find the decimal point in the dividend. Put the decimal point in the quotient directly above it. Then divide just as you would with whole numbers.

$35)\overline{94.85}$

$$
\begin{array}{r}
2.71 \\
35)\overline{94.85} \\
\underline{70} \\
248 \\
\underline{245} \\
35 \\
\underline{35} \\
\end{array}
$$

- **Dividing Decimals by Decimals**   To divide decimals by decimals, follow these steps: First, make the divisor a whole number. To do this move the decimal point to the right of the last digit. Then move the decimal point in the dividend the same number of places to the right. Put a decimal place in the quotient. Make sure it is directly above the decimal point in the dividend. Then, divide the same way you would divide a decimal by a whole number. (Remember: Write ending zeros in your dividend if you need to have more places.)

$$3.2\overline{)2.24}$$

$$3.2.\overline{)2.2.4}$$

$$\begin{array}{r} .7 \\ 32\overline{)22.4} \\ \underline{224} \\ 0 \end{array}$$

- **Dividing Decimals by 10, 100, 1,000**   You follow almost the same steps to divide decimals by 10, 100, or 1,000, that you follow when you multiply them. The difference is that you move the decimal point one place to the <u>left</u> for each zero. If you need help, read Basic Multiplication Facts in Appendix D again.

- **Rounding Decimals**   Rounding decimals can help you estimate an answer. Mixed numbers with decimals larger than .5 (or .50, or .500) can be rounded to the next larger whole number. Mixed numbers with decimals smaller than .5 can be left as is.

6.867 can be rounded to 7

6.324 can be rounded to 6

$12.14 can be rounded to $12.00

- **Changing Decimals to Fractions**   To change decimals to fractions, follow these steps: Use the digits of the decimal as the numerator. Count the number of places in the decimal. If the decimal has 1 place after the decimal point the denominator will be 10. If the decimal has 2 places after the decimal point, the denominator will be 100. If the decimal has 3 places after the decimal point, the denominator will be 1,000.

$.3 = \frac{3}{10}$

$.03 = \frac{3}{100}$

$.003 = \frac{3}{1,000}$

Remember: $.30 = .3$
so that $.30 = \frac{3}{100} = \frac{3}{10}$

- **Changing Fractions to Decimals**   To change fractions to decimals, follow these steps: First, divide 100 by the denominator. Then multiply the numerator by the quotient. Place the decimal two places to the right.

$$\frac{3}{5} = .\underline{\hspace{2cm}}$$

$$\begin{array}{r} 20 \\ 5\overline{)100} \end{array}$$

$$\begin{array}{r} 20 \\ \times\ 3 \\ \hline 60. \end{array}$$

$$\frac{3}{5} = .60$$

- **Estimating Decimals**   Rounding decimals will help you estimate answers. To round decimals follow these steps: First, look at the digit in the hundreds place. If that digit is 5 or more, add 1 to the tens place. If the digit is less than 5, make no changes in the tens place. You can drop all the digits to the right of the tens (or hundreds) place. Remember: When working with money, always keep two decimal places, writing in zeros when necessary.

2.56 $\longrightarrow$ more than 5

2.56 rounds to 2.6

2.54 $\longrightarrow$ less than 5

2.54 rounds to 2.5 or $2.50

3.426 $\longrightarrow$ less than 5

3.426 rounds to 3.4 or $3.40

Appendix I: Abbreviations in Ads

Here are some shortened words that you will find in ads and signs.

A

adlt   adults only (no children)

AEK   all electric kitchen (electric stove and refrigerator)

aft.   after

A.M.   morning (between midnight and noon)

amt.   amount

apt.   apartment

avail. immed. or *immed. occup.*   available immediately; immediate occupancy (you could move in now)

B

bath or *bthrm.* or *BA*   bathroom

bdrm   bedroom

C

chld. or *chldrn.*   children

clos. or *clst.*   closet

conv. or *conven.*   convenient (near)

cozy   small

cpt. or *carp.*   carpet

cyl.   cylinder

D

dep.   deposit

din. rm.   dining room

drps.   drapes

E

elev.   elevator

excel.   excellent

F

FP   fireplace

frig. or *refrig.*   refrigerator

furn.   furnished

G

gar.   garage

I

incl.   includes

K

kit.   kitchen

L

laund. or *lndy.*   laundry room in the building

lb.   pound

lge.   large

liv. rm.   living room

M

med.   medium

mess.   message (call and leave message)

mgr.   manager (the man or woman who runs the building)

mo.   month

mod.   modern (new or new looking)

mph   miles per hour

N

new. dec.   newly decorated (with new drapes, carpets, paint, and so on)

no. or *#*   number

nr.   near

O

op.   operated

oz.   ounce

P

pet OK   you could have pets in the apartment

pkg.   package

P.M.   afternoon or evening (between noon and midnight)

pvt.   private

Q

qts.   quarts

R

reg.   regular, regularly

req'd.   required

S

sec.   security

shop. or *shops.*   stores or shopping

sing. or *sngl.*   single people (no children)

sm.   small

spac.   spacious (large rooms)

studio   a small apartment with no bedroom

stv.   stove

sup. or *super.*   superintendent (the man or woman who runs the building)

T

trans. or *transp.*   transportation (such as a bus or train)

U

unfurn.   unfurnished

utils. incl.   utilities included (gas, water, and electric bills are a part of the rent)

$... up   the rents start with this amount, and some are more than this

W

wk. up   walk up (no elevator, just stairs)

w/   with

w/w cpt. or *w/w/carp.*   wall-to-wall carpet

Y

yr.   year

Basic Math Charts

Basic Addition Chart

1 + 0 1	1 + 1 2	1 + 2 3	1 + 3 4	1 + 4 5	1 + 5 6	1 + 6 7	1 + 7 8	1 + 8 9	1 + 9 10
2 + 0 2	2 + 1 3	2 + 2 4	2 + 3 5	2 + 4 6	2 + 5 7	2 + 6 8	2 + 7 9	2 + 8 10	2 + 9 11
3 + 0 3	3 + 1 4	3 + 2 5	3 + 3 6	3 + 4 7	3 + 5 8	3 + 6 9	3 + 7 10	3 + 8 11	3 + 9 12
4 + 0 4	4 + 1 5	4 + 2 6	4 + 3 7	4 + 4 8	4 + 5 9	4 + 6 10	4 + 7 11	4 + 8 12	4 + 9 13
5 + 0 5	5 + 1 6	5 + 2 7	5 + 3 8	5 + 4 9	5 + 5 10	5 + 6 11	5 + 7 12	5 + 8 13	5 + 9 14
6 + 0 6	6 + 1 7	6 + 2 8	6 + 3 9	6 + 4 10	6 + 5 11	6 + 6 12	6 + 7 13	6 + 8 14	6 + 9 15
7 + 0 7	7 + 1 8	7 + 2 9	7 + 3 10	7 + 4 11	7 + 5 12	7 + 6 13	7 + 7 14	7 + 8 15	7 + 9 16
8 + 0 8	8 + 1 9	8 + 2 10	8 + 3 11	8 + 4 12	8 + 5 13	8 + 6 14	8 + 7 15	8 + 8 16	8 + 9 17
9 + 0 9	9 + 1 10	9 + 2 11	9 + 3 12	9 + 4 13	9 + 5 14	9 + 6 15	9 + 7 16	9 + 8 17	9 + 9 18

Basic Subtraction Chart

9 −0 9	9 −1 8	9 −2 7	9 −3 6	9 −4 5	9 −5 4	9 −6 3	9 −7 2	9 −8 1	9 −9 0
8 −0 8	8 −1 7	8 −2 6	8 −3 5	8 −4 4	8 −5 3	8 −6 2	8 −7 1	8 −8 0	
7 −0 7	7 −1 6	7 −2 5	7 −3 4	7 −4 3	7 −5 2	7 −6 1	7 −7 0		
6 −0 6	6 −1 5	6 −2 4	6 −3 3	6 −4 2	6 −5 1	6 −6 0			
5 −0 5	5 −1 4	5 −2 3	5 −3 2	5 −4 1	5 −5 0				
4 −0 4	4 −1 3	4 −2 2	4 −3 1	4 −4 0					
3 −0 3	3 −1 2	3 −2 1	3 −3 0						
2 −0 2	2 −1 1	2 −2 0							
1 −0 1	1 −1 0								

Multiplication Table

Look at the multiplication chart below. It is easy to find the product of any two numbers on the chart. Find one number in the first column going down. Find the second number in the top row going across. Move across from the first column and down from the top row. The box in which the row and column meet contains the product of the two numbers.

1	2	3	4	5	6	7	8	9	10
2	4	6	8	10	12	14	16	18	20
3	6	9	12	15	18	21	24	27	30
4	8	12	16	20	24	28	32	36	40
5	10	15	20	25	30	35	40	45	50
6	12	18	24	30	36	42	48	54	60
7	14	21	28	35	42	49	56	63	70
8	16	24	32	40	48	56	64	72	80
9	18	27	36	45	54	63	72	81	90
10	20	30	40	50	60	70	80	90	100

Division Table

Look at the division chart below. It is easy to find the quotient of any two numbers on the chart. Find the divisor in the first column going down. Move across that row until you come to the dividend you want. Then move up that column until you get to the top row. The number in the box of the top row is the quotient.

1	2	3	4	5	6	7	8	9	10
2	4	6	8	10	12	14	16	18	20
3	6	9	12	15	18	21	24	27	30
4	8	12	16	20	24	28	32	36	40
5	10	15	20	25	30	35	40	45	50
6	12	18	24	30	36	42	48	54	60
7	14	21	28	35	42	49	56	63	70
8	16	24	32	40	48	56	64	72	80
9	18	27	36	45	54	63	72	81	90
10	20	30	40	50	60	70	80	90	100

Decimals to Percentages Chart

.01 = 1%	.11 = 11%	.21 = 21%	.31 = 31%	.41 = 41%	.51 = 51%	.61 = 61%	.71 = 71%	.81 = 81%	.91 = 91%
.02 = 2%	.12 = 12%	.22 = 22%	.32 = 32%	.42 = 42%	.52 = 52%	.62 = 62%	.72 = 72%	.82 = 82%	.92 = 92%
.03 = 3%	.13 = 13%	.23 = 23%	.33 = 33%	.43 = 43%	.53 = 53%	.63 = 63%	.73 = 73%	.83 = 83%	.93 = 93%
.04 = 4%	.14 = 14%	.24 = 24%	.34 = 34%	.44 = 44%	.54 = 54%	.64 = 64%	.74 = 74%	.84 = 84%	.94 = 94%
.05 = 5%	.15 = 15%	.25 = 25%	.35 = 35%	.45 = 45%	.55 = 55%	.65 = 65%	.75 = 75%	.85 = 85%	.95 = 95%
.06 = 6%	.16 = 16%	.26 = 26%	.36 = 36%	.46 = 46%	.56 = 56%	.66 = 66%	.76 = 76%	.86 = 86%	.96 = 96%
.07 = 7%	.17 = 17%	.27 = 27%	.37 = 37%	.47 = 47%	.57 = 57%	.67 = 67%	.77 = 77%	.87 = 87%	.97 = 97%
.08 = 8%	.18 = 18%	.28 = 28%	.38 = 38%	.48 = 48%	.58 = 58%	.68 = 68%	.78 = 78%	.88 = 88%	.98 = 98%
.09 = 9%	.19 = 19%	.29 = 29%	.39 = 39%	.49 = 49%	.59 = 59%	.69 = 69%	.79 = 79%	.89 = 89%	.99 = 99%
.1 = 10%	.2 = 20%	.3 = 30%	.4 = 40%	.5 = 50%	.6 = 60%	.7 = 70%	.8 = 80%	.9 = 90%	

Index

Rent,
    budgeting for, 106-108
    computing affordable, 106-108
    deposits, 105, 111-112, 118
Rental,
    application, 105, 111-112
    terms, 113-114
Retail, 173, 183-184, 194, 210-211

S

Salary, 37-38
    deductions from, 53-66
    monthly, 37, 40-50
    weekly, 37, 41-50
    yearly, 38, 40-50
Sales,
    ads for, 181, 185
    calendar, 190-192
    prices, 181-185
    storewide clearance, 189
Sales tax, *See* Tax
Savings,
    budgeting for, 7, 17-22
    types of accounts, 78-82
Security deposit, 111-112
Shipping and handling charges, 196-202
Shopping,
    for bargains, 190-192
    for food, 137-143, 147-150
    for furnishings, 122-129
    for household necessities, 129-131
    for personal items, 173-176, 179-181
Signature,
    as endorsement, 87
    authorized, 87
    card, 87, 100
Social Security (FICA), 54-66
Statement,
    bank, 87, 94-100
    billing, 232-233, 247-248
    earnings, 53, 57-59
Stores,
    catalogs from, 194-203
    discount, 193-194
    factory-outlet, 189, 193-194

T

Tax,
    federal, 51-66
    sales, 201-203, 211
    state, 54, 57–59
Time card, 37, 41-42, 50
Time clock, 41, 50
Tips, 45-46, 48, 50
Tires, 229-231
Trade-in, 213, 218
Transfer of budget items, 17, 20, 27
Travel,
    budgeting for, 293-299
    costs of, 293-299
    lodging, 287, 293-294, 300
    mileage, 287-295, 300
    planning for, 287-300

U

Union,
    credit, 54, 58
    dues for, 54-55, 58
United Fund, 54, 57-58
U.S. RDA, 144-145
Utilities, 3

V

Variable expenses, 3, 10-14
Vehicle, *See* Car

W

Wages, 37, 44
    hourly, 37, 42-43
    weekly, 37, 41-50
    overtime, 37, 43-45
Wants, 27-32
Warranties, 223, 230-231
Wholesale prices, 173, 183-185, 210-211